TOP MARK

HORSE RACING

SYSTEM .

WRITTEN BY PROFESSIONAL

GAMBLER ANTHONY GIBSON

CONTENTS

INTRODUCTION

The idea for the Top Mark system was born when I was introduced through a friend to a tipster who lives and operates in Dublin. Since we were introduced we have remained pretty good friends and stay in touch on a day to day basis, he has visited me in the town where I live I have yet to find time to visit him in Dublin but plan to do so shortly. My friend used to be a bookmaker and worked for all of the top high street bookmaker as an odds compiler, shop manager and accounts manager. He knows the bookmaking industry inside out, Ill health forced him to quit and he turned his knowledge to running a very successful tipping service, one he still runs today and makes very good returns for his clients. We were asked to work on a project together and exchange ideas to see if we could come up with a successful tipping line for which we would be paid to run by a third party.

My friend will not strike a bet unless it has been backed in the markets this is something he picked up whilst working in the industry and it makes perfect sense. Each morning he would send me a list of horses that had been backed overnight, I generally looked at the betting market movers around 9.30am each day as part of my own form study, so to me it made perfect sense to compare the overnight market movers with the morning market movers to see if the same horses were still being shortened up in the betting markets, from this shortlist I would then look at other factors Jockeys, Trainers, both their recent form, percentage when they teamed up, percentage at the tracks, horses form, ratings Racing Post Ratings, Timeform Ratings etc. etc.

Whilst we were having some initial success and our joint venture was doing well finding winners for ourselves and paying clients, I was not convinced the evening market movers were having a great bearing on the overall results and because the tipping service had become so time consuming it was detracting me from my own strategies and effecting my own profits so we decided not to proceed any further with this venture.

Over time I kept revisiting the market movers as for me they have always been a great source of winners, if you have a horse that is working well at home and looks to have a great chance of winning its next engagement are you going to let it go unbacked? I don't know many owners who don't like to have a bit of a flutter and many multiple owners are renowned for having a tilt at the ring such as JP McManus and Barney Curley to name just a couple.

Another area that produces lots of winners are ratings, I have used rating to great effect ever since I started betting on horses the ratings I initially started using before the advent of computers were very time consuming to use but working the ratings out manually taught me a lot about handicapping and how they were framed and well handicapped runners all part and parcel of backing winners. I have used many more ratings since including Raceform, Timeform and the Racing Post Ratings (RPR) it is the latter I use now with this method as I do believe when the Racing Post have a cleat top rated runner then its certainly worth delving into. The combination of a horse that has been well backed and Clear RPR runners form the basis of this method, a simple method in itself but endless hours of research to get me to this point, now on with the method itself.

THE METHOD EXPLAINED

The results derived to date using this method do not involve any form study whatsoever. If you are into racing the idea of using such a method may seem rather silly, but I have found over the years that sometimes a very simplistic approach to racing can pay off if it is based upon sound principles. I know people who are quite successful following jockeys / trainers etc. without applying any form to their approaches and simply leave it up to the jockeys agents to find them the winners or the trainers to place their horses in the correct types of race, and I see nothing wrong with such an approach whatsoever. When I first started to research the top mark method I threw lots of criteria into the mix for me to come up with selections, as the research continued and I started to collate the results some of the criteria I was using could be discarded, in fact it was clouding the bare facts of the method, and costing me lots of money in the process. The initial criteria I used is listed below:-

Trainer – Course form – Current form

Jockey – Course form – Current form

Horse – Course form – Current form – Ratings – Timeform and Racing Post Ground and going requirements

Betting – had the horse been backed? and position in market

From the above information I devised a set of ratings for each element for every horse running on the day in mainly handicap races the horse achieving most of the criteria with the Top Mark rating was generally a bet.

This was a very time-consuming exercise and one I didn't take on lightly, of course if you are having success operating such a method then the time put in is irrelevant as it is the profits you are taking out that count and believe me I was making excellent profits!! I suppose you could argue that what I was doing was basic form study, but was actually compiling a set of rating based upon this form study.

As you go along using a method you are making mental notes of what information is useful and what is not, for instance I realized that the trainers current form counted more than course form, which meant that I could drop that side of the method. The Jockeys course form was more relevant than his current form. Racing post ratings were more accurate than Timeform when it came to finding well handicapped horses and produced more winners from their top rated runners. The position in the market didn't matter at all it was the fact the horse had been backed early morning that counted and on and on it goes. I realized that the strict criteria I was using was actually costing me winners, lots of winners at good prices most days of the week and this was affecting the potentially very good profits I could be making by basically combining just two of the factors mentioned above in the original criteria I had set out for myself.

What I am stating is that the method I now use has been born out of a long painstaking series of research and development over a period of a couple of years, it is not just some crazy idea I have made up and has not happened accidently although the method now is very simplistic but very effective. It did not start out being so, in fact just the opposite but once you see and understand the two elements involved in the process I think you will start to comprehend how it evolved and why it works and should continue to work and return decent profits. And by the way the price tag of this system means I won't be selling many copies so you should be able to carry on replicating the profits made to date.

THE SELECTION METHOD EXPLAINED

STEP 1

Go to the website www.attheraces.com/marketmovers save this site on your laptop for easy access each morning

When you click on the site you are looking for the Market movers section which will bring up the following page. This is a list of meetings taking place on this particular day

Today the 15th of August 2018 there are meetings at Beverley, Gowran Park (IRE) Kempton, Newton Abbott, Salisbury, Worcester

Straight away put a line through GOWRAN PARK (IRE) the (IRE) in brackets

means this is an Irish meeting and we have no need to include any Irish racing in the method as we will have enough to concentrate on with UK RACING ALONE. I HAVE NOT RESEARCHED RESULTS FROM IRELAND SO LEAVE IT ALONE. This leaves us with the five meetings.

Beverly and Salisbury are flat turf meetings

Kempton is a flat all-weather meeting (artificial surface)

Newton Abbott and Worcester are turf jumps meetings
It does not matter what type of meeting we encounter i.e. Jumps, Flat, Flat all weather, as the method works well on all types of tracks, under both codes flat and jumps and all types of going and surfaces, so no need to worry about any of this at all.

STEP 2

We now need to look at all of the individual meetings to see what is being backed. By this I mean the market movers on the attheraces website. **The time I look at these movers AND THIS IS VERY IMPORTANT is between 9.30am and 9.45am** the method has not been tested using market movers at any other time of the day and I know form past experience that this is the best time to check the market movers

Newton Abbot

Top 10 Steamers for Newton Abbot

Horse Name	Race	Last Price	1st Show
Madame Vogue	New 16:50	10/1	20/1
Torhousemuir	New 16:20	7/1	10/1
Cultivator	New 14:50	3/1	3.5/1
Marettimo	New 13:50	5/1	6/1
Scorpion Star	New 15:50	8.5/1	11/1
American History	New 13:50	3/1	3.33/1
Eric The Third	New 16:20	4/1	4.5/1
Delirant	New 13:50	1.75/1	1.88/1
Voodoo Doll	New 14:50	4.5/1	5/1
Cracker Factory	New 14:20	.18/1	.2/1

STEP 3

From the above list of Market Movers you need to note down any market mover that is in a race where the Racing Post have a **CLEAR TOP RATED RUNNER IN THE FIELD**

Note in the above race there are three market movers in the field that we have transferred from the At the races Market Movers page, but the only horse we are interested in from a selection point of view is **No 10 MARETTIMO** Note the black dot on the race card which signifies it is not only top rated but **CLEAR TOP RATED** no other horse in the field is marked with this **BLACK DOT**

Note in the above race there is just the one market mover in the field, so the only horse we are interested in from a selection point of view is **No 1 CRACKER FACTORY** Note the black dot on the race card which signifies it is not only top rated but **CLEAR TOP RATED** no other horse in the field is marked with this **BLACK DOT**

Salisbury

Top 10 Steamers for Salisbury

Horse Name	Race	Last Price	1st Show
Champs De Reves	Sal 16:10	2/1	3.33/1
Chain Of Daisies	Sal 15:40	2.25/1	3.5/1
Dirty Rascal	Sal 14:10	1.63/1	2/1
Tahreek	Sal 15:10	1.88/1	2.25/1
Signore Piccolo	Sal 14:40	3.33/1	4/1
May Remain	Sal 14:40	8/1	11/1
Crystal Casque	Sal 16:40	4.5/1	5.5/1
Face Like Thunder	Sal 16:40	7.5/1	10/1
Tinos	Sal 16:10	2.25/1	2.5/1
Savaanah	Sal 15:40	9/1	12/1

CONTINUE THIS PROCESS FOR EVERY MEETING RUN ON THE DAY

2.40 S H Jones Wines Handicap (Class 4)
RACE 2   Winner £5,757.41   RUK   5f

£10,100 guaranteed For 3yo + Rated 61-80 (also open to such horses rated 81 and 82, such horses rated 60 and below are also eligible - see Standard Conditions) Weights highest weight, 4yo + 9st 10lb; 3yo 9st 7lb Minimum Weight 8-5, 3-y-o 8-2 Penalties after August 4th, each race won 6lb Weight for age 3 from 4yo + 7lb Delagate This Lord's Handicap Mark 78 Entries 14 pay £40 Penalty value 1st £5,757.41 2nd £1,713.25 3rd £856.18 4th £429.00 5th £300 6th £300

1 (3) -733256 **DELAGATE THIS LORD** 21 BF 0s S1 F1   4 9-9
  b g Delegator-Lady Filly   *William Carson
  Michael Attwater Mrs M S Teversham   90

2 (6) -459121 **SECRETFACT** 12 0s S2 F1   5 9-8
  br g Sakhee's Secret-Matereollect   Pat Cosgrave
  Malcolm Saunders Premier Conservatory Roofs   88

3 (1) 154-447 **MAY REMAIN** 18 Ds S1   3 9-7
  b g Mayson-Ultimate Best   David Probert   8/1
  Paul Cole PJ Racing Wright/Higley/Jones/Wilcock   89

4 (2) 3-54463 **SIGNORE PICCOLO** 16   np1 7 9-7
  b g Piccolo-Piccola Cativo   David Egan   100/30
  David Loughnane Mike Ae   02

5 (5) 22136-5 **SWING OUT SISTER** (IRE) 61 B1   3 9-1
  b f Kodiac-Dance Club   *Adam Kirby
  Clive Cox S R Hope & S W Barrow   87

6 (4) 7-03211 **LOOK SURPRISED** (6ex) 9 D2 F2   5 9-1
  ch m Kier Park-Clonda   CB1   William Cox(5)
  Roger Teal Starting Gate Racing   88

2017 (8 ran) Waseem Faris (4) Ken Cunningham-Brown 8 9-6 14/1   Pat Dobbs OR76

No 4 SIGNORE PICCOLO IS THE
SELECTION ABOVE

No 3 CHAIN OF DAISIES IS THE
SELECTION ABOVE

3.40 British Stallion Studs EBF
Upavon Fillies' Stakes (Listed Race)
RACE 4   (Class 1)   RUK
Winner £31,190.50   (1m 1f 201y)1m2f

£56,000 guaranteed For 3yo + fillies & mares which are LBF eligible Weights 3yo 8st 8lb; 4yo + 9st 2lb Penalties After 2017, a winner of a Group 3 race 3lb, of a Group 2 race 5lb, of a Group 1 race 7lb Weight for age 3 from 4yo + 8lb Entries 17 pay £350 Penalty value 1st £31,190.50 2nd £11,825 3rd £5,918 4th £2,948 5th £1,479.50 6th £742.50

1 (4) -114562 **PROMISING RUN** (USA) 36 BF S1   p5 9-7
  b m Hard Spun-Aviacion   Pat Cosgrave
  Saeed Bin Suroor Godolphin   115

2 (7) 15-6498 **BILLESDON BESS** 14 B1 S2 F2   4 9-2
  br f Dick Turpin-Coplow   C1 CB2   *Dane O'Neill
  Richard Hannon Pall Mall Partners & Partners   114

3 (1) 6231-60 **CHAIN OF DAISIES** 1/2 D1   6 9-2
  b m Rail Link-Puya   Harry Bentley   9/4
  Henry Candy Glasenfield Ltd   122

4 (3) 11320-8 **LUIRE** (IRE) 187 S1   4 9-2
  gr f Dark Angel-Glitter Baby   *Adam Kirby
  Clive Cox7 Michael Johnson & John Law   110

5 (9) 2-98416 **MIA TESORO** (IRE) 4/2 B1 F4   n5 9-2
  b m Danehill Dancer-Souter's Sister   Stevie Donohoe
  Charlie Fellowes Denro Pearson   112

6 (8) 12229-6 **PLEASANT SURPRISE** (IRE) 19 F1   4 9-2
  b f Mastercraftsman-Ibiza Dream   Jamie Spencer
  Luca Cumani Gerry Mordaunt & Partners   116

7 (5) 6-13 **CRYSTAL HOPE** 58 BF D1 S1   3 8-8
  ch f Nathaniel-Crystal Etoile   *Ryan Moore
  Sir Michael Stoute Sir Evelyn De Rothschild   111

8 (2) -221525 **RASIMA** 19 F1   3 8-8
  gr f Ilhavy-Raushen   Andrea Atzeni
  Roger Varian Nurlan Bizakov   112

9 (6) 2-21112 **SAVAANAH** (IRE) 14 B1   3 8-8
  b f Golden Times-Tancouma   CB1   David Probert   9/1
  Roger Charlton Prince A A Faisal   108

2017 (9 ran) Billesdon Bess (2) Richard Hannon 3 8-9 6/1   Hollie Doyle RPR102

Beverley

Top 10 Steamers for Beverley

Horse Name	Race	Last Price	1st Show
Our Little Pony	Bev 17:00	3/1	5.5/1
Dream Poet	Bev 14:30	6.5/1	14/1
Everything For You	Bev 15:30	4/1	6/1
Kingson	Bev 14:30	1.5/1	1.75/1
Golconda Prince	Bev 16:00	5.5/1	7.5/1
Silver Crescent	Bev 16:30	3/1	3.5/1
Ideal Candy	Bev 16:00	3.33/1	4/1
Blue Reflection	Bev 16:00	3.33/1	4/1
Zihaam	Bev 16:30	9/1	12/1
Harbour Pilot	Bev 16:00	10/1	14/1

No 6 KINGSON IS THE SELECTION FROM THE ABOVE RACE

No 5 BLUE REFLECTION IS THE SELECTION FROM THE ABOVE RACE

Worcester

Top 10 Steamers for Worcester

Horse Name	Race	Last Price	1st Show
So Sorry Sarah	wor 18:50	1.75/1	2.25/1
Outrageous Romana	wor 18:50	4.5/1	6/1
Cotton Club	wor 20:20	1.5/1	1.75/1
Massini's Dream	wor 20:20	2.5/1	3/1
Boss Mans Ladder	wor 17:20	6.5/1	8/1
Undisputed	wor 18:50	8/1	10/1
Mr Caffrey	wor 19:50	3/1	3.33/1
Dr Dunraven	wor 17:50	2.5/1	2.75/1
Starcrossed	wor 19:50	4/1	4.5/1
Desirable Court	wor 19:20	.33/1	.36/1

No 7 OUTRAGEOUS ROMANA IS THE SELECTION FROM THE ABOVE RACE

No 3 DESIRABLE COURT IS THE SELECTION FROM THE ABOVE RACE

No 1 COTTON CLUB IS THE SELECTION FROM THE ABOVE RACE

No 8 MR CAFFREY IS THE SELECTION FROM THE ABOVE RACE

Kempton

Top 10 Steamers for Kempton

Horse Name	Race	Last Price	1st Show
Trogon	Kmp 20:00	8/1	12/1
Rock'n Gold	Kmp 21:00	8/1	12/1
I Am Magical	Kmp 18:00	5.5/1	8/1
Querelle	Kmp 18:00	7.5/1	11/1
Shikoba	Kmp 19:00	7/1	9/1
Bird For Life	Kmp 21:00	5/1	6/1
Mr Fox	Kmp 17:30	14/1	20/1
Pot Luck	Kmp 17:30	2.75/1	3/1
Perfect Hustler	Kmp 20:30	1.75/1	1.88/1
Jumeirah Street	Kmp 19:00	1.88/1	2/1

7.00
RACE 4

Breeders Backing Racing EBF **RUK**
Fillies' Novice Stakes (Div I) (Class 5)
Winner £5,175.20   **7f AW**

No 8 JUMEIRAH IS THE SELECTION FROM THE ABOVE RACE

Note: It does not matter how many horses are backed in a particular race at this stage of our research to become a selection all we are interested in is the fact that

1- **THE HORSE HAS BEEN BACKED (MORNING MARKET MOVER ATTHERACES WEBSITE at 9.30 to 9.45am)**

2- **THE HORSE IS CLEAR TOP RATED BY THE RACING POST RATINGS (RPR)**

STEP 4

BACKING THE SELECTIONS

This part of the method is almost as important as the selection method itself, the best way to back the selections is online with a best odds guaranteed bookmaker, by this I mean a bookmaker who will offer the best odds on the horse regardless of whether the horse shortens up in the betting after you have backed it or lengthens in the betting again after you have placed your bet.

Example:-

You find a selection in the morning go onto your bookmakers platform and place a bet on the horse you will note the odds and the potential returns whilst you are in the process of doing this. Just say at the time you place your bet the horse is a 2/1 chance (3.0 decimal) when the race is run the horse is backed further into 1/1 (2.0) if it wins the bookmaker will pay you out at 2/1 so you have gained a point by backing at BOG (best odds guaranteed). On the other hand if the horse had drifted after you had backed it 2/1 (3.0) out to 3/1 (4.0) the bookmaker will pay the best odds which are 3/1 so again you have gained a point. Basically you cannot lose unless the selection loses and believe me many of the selections will be backed into shorter odds than you took and many will drift so a win-win situation for us punters and these are the types of situations you need to exploit. The choice of bookmaker is entirely yours. Do your research to find the bookmakers offering BOG along with other bonuses if you sign up with them e.g. Free bets, weekly bonuses etc.

THAT IS BASICALLY THE CRUX OF THE METHOD BUT I NOW WANT TO POINT OUT ANOTHER PART OF THE SELECTION PROCESS WHICH MAY BE OF INTEREST TO YOU WHEN YOU EXAMINE THE RESULTS TO DATE AS THIS EXTRA METHOD CAN CUT DOWN ON THE BETS YOU PLACE EACH DAY OR CAN ENHANCE THE PROFITS MADE USING THE BASIC METHOD SHOWN EXPLAINED SO FAR

THE ONE HORSE BOOK

Here I want to take the method a stage further, note there is no extra work involved in doing so, it is simply an observation I made when noting the results to date and another angle to how you could operate or stake the method. This further observation has basically increased my earnings from the method by 2/3rds but it does involve increasing your stakes (something I will go into later) on these qualifying selections. Another positive too is you may well want to use this instead of the initial method I have explained if you don't like to back lots of selections per day which the basic method does have from time to time. Using this One horse book method will cut down on selections by over 50% yet only cost you about 1/3rd of the profits so realistically you could stake higher on these types of selections.

Again note the screenshots we took on this days racing below:-

Of all the races mentioned in the first part of the method ONE HORSE BOOK SELECTIONS are exactly as stated

In The 2.20 Race at Newton Abbott no1 Cracker Factory is CLEAR TOP RATED with RPR and is the ONLY HORSE BACKED IN THE RACE i.e. A ONE HORSE BOOK

In The 7.20 Race at Worcester no3 Cracker Factory is CLEAR TOP RATED with RPR and is the ONLY HORSE BACKED IN THE RACE i.e. A ONE HORSE BOOK

RESULTS FROM THE FULL DAYS SELECTIONS

1:50 ARCHIVE PLAYLISTS AVAILABLE ON attheraces.com MAIDEN HURDLE (4)

1st 4. DELIRANT (FR) 9/4

2nd 7. WINTER SPICE (IRE) 12/1

3rd 1. AULD SOD (IRE) 100/1

15 ran. NRs: VANDERBILT (IRE). Hurdles: 9.

J: Tom Scudamore

T: David Pipe

Our first selection in the first race was unplaced

2:20 DOWNLOAD THE FREE AT THE RACES APP JUVENILE HURDLE (3)

1st f 1. CRACKER FACTORY 1/8 f

2nd 3. VENTURA MAGIC 6/1

All 6 ran. Hurdles: 8.

J: Daryl Jacob

T: Alan King

Our second selection won at very restrictive odds of 1/8 we took 1/5 at best odds so a fraction gained on the SP of 0.08

2:40 S H JONES WINES HANDICAP (4)

1st ⬤ 4. SIGNORE PICCOLO 5/2

2nd ⬤ 1. DELAGATE THIS LORD 5/1

All 6 ran.

J: David Egan

T: David Loughnane

Our third selection won at 5/2 SP note we took the 100/30 at best odds so we have gained another fraction on the SP of 0.8

3:40 BRITISH STALLION STUDS EBF UPAVON FILLIES' STAKES (Listed) (1)

1st ⬤ 3. CHAIN OF DAISIES 7/4 f

2nd ⬤ 5. MIA TESORO (IRE) 16/1

3rd ⬤ 1. PROMISING RUN (USA) 5/1

8 ran. NRs: RASIMA.

J: Harry Bentley

T: Henry Candy

Our fourth selection was the easiest winner of the day and absolutely dotted up which to me shows the merit of this selection method. We took 9/4 at best odds and the horse won at 7/4 so 0.5 pinched form the bookies again

2:30 BEVERLEY FLEMINGATE SHOPPING
CENTRE EBF NOVICE STAKES (5)

1st 2. **DREAM POET 8/1**

2nd 1. BALANCE OF POWER 9/1

3rd 9. SAMEEM (IRE) 20/1

All 11 ran.

J: Jack Garritty

T: Jedd O'Keeffe

Our fifth selection was a bitter disappointment finishing out of the frame

4:00 OUTFIT AT FLEMINGATE HANDICAP
(5)

1st 3. **WEATHER FRONT (USA) 11/4**
f

2nd 8. VENTURA CREST (IRE) 8/1

3rd 6. IDEAL CANDY (IRE) 3/1

8 ran. NRs: WESTWARD HO (IRE) TAKE A
TURN (IRE).

J: Jamie Gormley (3)

T: Karen McLintock

Our sixth selection again was unplaced

6:50 myracing.com FOR FREE BETS AND TIPS MARES' HANDICAP HURDLE (4)

1st ✗ 7. OUTRAGEOUS ROMANA (IRE) 3/1 f

2nd 9. RUBYS CUBE 40/1

3rd 3. NORTHERN BEAU (IRE) 9/1

10 ran. NRs: STARLIT NIGHT. Hurdles: 12.

J: Edward Austin (7)

T: John O'Shea

Our seventh selection won quite easily at a good price of 3/1 but we got 9/2 taking best odds so another gain on the SP here of 1.5 points

7:20 R&A MASON, HEATING & ELECTRICAL SERVICES NOVICES' HURDLE (Qualifier) (4)

1st 1. BUGSIE MALONE (IRE) 5/1

2nd 5. SETTIMO MILANESE (IRE) 9/4

5 ran. NRs: WINGSOFREDEMPTION (IRE). Hurdles: 12.

J: Tom Cannon

T: Chris Gordon

Our eighth selection on the day was turned over at 1/3 incredibly short not to win and a very disappointing result

7:50 FOLLOW @myracingtips ON
INSTAGRAM HANDICAP HURDLE (4)

1st 3. **MAJESTIC MOLL (IRE) 7/2**

2nd 8. MR CAFFREY 5/2 f

3rd 2. REDEMPTION SONG (IRE) 3/1

All 10 ran. Hurdles: 10.

J: Adam Wedge

T: Emma Lavelle

Our ninth selection was placed behind an easy winner and never looked like winning

8:20 myracing.com FOR FREE TIPS EVERY
DAY MAIDEN HURDLE (Qualifier) (5)

1st 2. **CUL DE POULE 40/1**

2nd 13. MASSINI'S DREAM 5/2

3rd 5. HEYDOUR (IRE) 10/1

12 ran. NRs: BIT MORE (IRE) MISKIN.
Hurdles: 10.

J: Andrew Tinkler

T: Martin Keighley

Our 10th selection was another beaten favourite that never looked in the hunt

7:00 BREEDERS BACKING RACING EBF
FILLIES' NOVICE STAKES (5) (D.I)

1st 8. JUMEIRAH STREET (USA) 5/2
f

2nd 4. DUCHESS OF AVON 3/1

3rd 7. INVINCIBLE PEACE 33/1

All 10 ran.

J: Jamie Spencer
T: James Tate

Our last selection won for us and again we have taken money from the bookies here by making use of their generosity in giving us BOG we backed at 15/8 and the horse finished up at an SP of 5/2 +0.63 of a point pinched

After a quite a busy day of betting we had 11 selections which to be fair is a little daunting, we had winners at 1/5, 100/30, 9/4, 9/2 and 5/2 and 6 losers making a profit on the day of 6.75 points

The One Horse Book bets had a winner and a loser making a loss of 0.8 points so if we had combined the two methods we would have made a total profit on the day of 5.95 points

Combining the two methods obviously increases our outlay as it effectively means we have two points rather than a single point on the One Horse Book selections.

Your options staking this method is to simply back all selections from what I call the TOPMARK method, or combine the two methods i.e. TOPMARK and the ONE HORSE BOOK selections which would increase your returns but also increase your stakes, or simply back the ONE HORSE BOOK SELECTIONS if you haven't an appetite for backing lots of selections each day

The TOPMARK method averages around 5 bets per day

The ONE HORSE BOOK method averages just under two selections per day, yet makes about 2/3rds of the overhaul profit of TOPMARK

HOW YOU STAKE THIS METHOD IS ENTIRELY UP TO YOU. I SEE NO REASON WHY YOU CANNOT STAKE BOTH METHODS IF YOU HAVE THE CORRECT BANK SIZE IN PLACE

TOPMARK = 100 Point bank

ONE HORSE BOOK = 40 point bank

COMBINED 140 point bank

Another area of the method you may want to explore is the following:-

As you are using the Racing Post Ratings either online or the paper version go to the Signpost pages of the post if online

https://www.racingpost.com/landing/digitalnewspaper/

MISCELLANEOUS

Signposts............ GB 22; IRE 63
Today's Trainers 22
Today's Jockeys.......................24
Trainerspot .... GB 24; IRE 63
Today's Flat Sires 25
Index to today's runners.......25

Signposts

Signposts include trainers, jockeys
& horses engaged today in Britain,
unless stated otherwise.
▶▶Current season plus four
▶▶Form in Britain and Ireland (and
point-to-point), plus European
Group races, under relevant code.

They are of interest for these what I call banker bets is the trainer and jockeys section listed below. The list contains Jockeys and trainers who have an extremely high strike rate when teaming up at a course and if they fit the criteria mentioned above I.E. Racing Post Top Rated and have been backed then I do believe these horses have a terrific chance of winning as the trainer has booked a jockey who rides well for the stable

BANKER BETS

Trainers & jockeys

▶▶ TRAINER-JOCKEY combinations with best % from at least three course wins

Ian Williams-Jim Crowley ...Donc**100%**
all Donc; trainer 17%; jockey 13%
Keith Dalgleish-Brian Hughes Kels **43%**
all Kels; trainer 32%; jockey 19%
Emma Lavelle-Daryl Jacob .Winc **38%**
all Winc; trainer 21%; jockey 24%
Paul Nicholls-Bryony Frost .Winc **38%**
all Winc; trainer 32%; jockey 15%
Paul Nicholls-Harry Cobden Winc **36%**
all Winc; trainer 32%; jockey 28%
Luca Cumani-Jamie Spencer Donc **35%**
all Donc; trainer 27%; jockey 20%
Richard Fahey-Sebastian Woods
....Donc **33%**
all Donc; trainer 10%; jockey 27%
Iain Jardine-Ross Chapman ..Kels **33%**
all Kels; trainer 18%; jockey 19%
Roger Varian-Andrea Atzeni Donc **30%**
all Donc; trainer 25%; jockey 26%
Lucinda Russell-Blair Campbell .
....Kels **29%**
all Kels; trainer 14%; jockey 26%

12122P- **IF YOU SAY RUN** (IRE) 231 S!   16 11-5
3   *b m Mahler-de Lissa*   7/4   Harry Cobden ⑭
Paul Nicholls | Highclere T'Bred Racing If You Say Run

BETTING FORECAST: 9-4 If You Say Run, **4** Litterale Ci, Little Miss Poet, **7** Grageelagh Girl, **8** Miss Crick, **10** G For Ginger, **12** Talent To Amuse, **20** Graceful Legend.

1st 3. If You Say Run 6/4F

Mahler - De Lissa (IRE) (Zaffaran
(USA))
Breeder Michael O'Regan
Owner Highclere T'Bred Racing If You
Say Run

2nd 1. Litterale Ci 4/1
3rd 6. Talent To Amuse 14/1

/11043- **PRESENT MAN** (IRE) ¹⁹⁶ **S1 F1** ₈ 11-12
1 b g Presenting-Glen's Gale C2 CD1
5/1 Bryony Frost(3)
Paul Nicholls Mr & Mrs Mark Woodhouse 154

BETTING FORECAST: 5 El Bandit, 11-2 Present Man, 7 Bigbadjohn,
10 Fingerontheswitch, 11 Captain Buck's, 12 Forever Field, Kings Lad, Sam Red,
14 Allelu Alleiula, Aunty Ann, Belmount, Ramses de Teillee, Sumkindofking,
16 On Demand, 25 Bestwork, Dancing Shadow.

1st 1. Present Man 5/1J

Presenting - Glen's Gale (IRE) (Strong
Gale (IRE))
Breeder Kenneth Parkhill
Owner Mr & Mrs Mark Woodhouse

2nd 10. Sumkindofking 10/1
3rd 15. Fingeronthes… 16/1
4th 11. Aunty Ann 16/1

Trainers & jockeys

▶▶ TRAINER-JOCKEY combinations with best % from at least three course wins

Nicky Henderson-Daryl Jacob Sand **54%**
all Sand; trainer 29%; jockey 31%

Fergal O'Brien-Paddy Brennan ..
....Sand **50%**
all Sand; trainer 38%; jockey 13%

Kim Bailey-David Bass ....Ffos **35%**
all Ffos; trainer 24%; jockey 34%

Philip Hobbs-Richard Johnson ...
....Sand **24%**
all Sand; trainer 16%; jockey 17%

Gary Moore-Jamie Moore ...Sand **22%**
all Sand; trainer 13%; jockey 24%

Sue Gardner-Lucy Gardner ...Ffos **20%**
all Ffos; trainer 17%; jockey 20%

Alan King-Wayne Hutchinson Sand **20%**
all Sand; trainer 17%; jockey 16%

David Pipe-Tom Scudamore .Ffos **20%**
all Ffos; trainer 14%; jockey 18%

Evan Williams-Adam Wedge Ffos **20%**
all Ffos; trainer 16%; jockey 17%

131121- **TERREFORT** (FR) ²¹²D1 S5 C1   5 11-8
2 *gr g Martaline-Vie de Reine*   4/6   Daryl Jacob 170
Nicky Henderson | Simon Munir & Isaac Souede

BETTING FORECAST: 4-6 Terrefort, 9-2 Elegant Escape, Thomas Patrick, 7 Coo Star Sivola.

4  2. **Terrefort** (FR) 4/6F

39 [49½]   5yo **11**st **8**lb **158**OR **73**TS **127**RPR —MR

T: Nicky Henderson   J: Daryl Jacob

Relating the original method to the additional information above will greatly cut down your bets but will mean you are backing the most solid of all the selections the method throws up. Good trainer / Jockey combination with a very high strike rate at the track, their runner being top rated and backed to do the business.

BACKERS MINDSET

I always include this section or similar in all of the publications I have produced to date and for a very good reason. If a method makes a profit I will guarantee most of the people that purchase and operate it after a short period will have given up on it or lose money following it, how can that be. Most punters I know are rule breakers and for reasons I fully understand, the method may stall or go backward for a period which brings on frustration for the user who wants to make his or her fortune in a short space of time so will throw the staking plan out of the window and chase losses etc. and simply play into the bookies hands by breaking the rules I have set out.

You may be fortunate and start following this method when we are in the process of having a good run and immediately add money to your bank, the opposite may happen and is very likely that you will start backing selections whilst a losing run occurs, this is why we need a bank and a sizable one to get us through these stick periods. To date the TOPMARK method is about 400 points in profit to £10 stakes £4000 in profit. The ONE HORSE BOOK method is about 220 points in profit, again to £10 stakes £2200 in profit, so a combined total of £6200 and this is over a period of about 14 months

Why have I seen people come and go on my website that have subscribed to this service? Its quite simple 1/ there may simply be too many bets 2/ they cannot make it pay because they are rule breakers, chasing losses, staking more on a loser than on a winner etc. etc. I am sure you know the score.

So here is what we must do. Put the recommended banks in place on your chosen bookmakers platform, note here that this bank is money that you have no other use for than to lose. You must be of the mindset that the money you place into your betting account is money already lost and this is always a possibility as past results do not guarantee future success. The banks you deposit determine the amount you can stake on each selection. I have stated that each selection should carry a one point stake and the bank for TOP MARK should be 100 points and for ONE HORSE BOOK SELECTIONS 40 points so if operating both methods a 140 point bank so a £1400 bank to stake to £10.

Work out your selections each morning and place your bets. Take the prices on offer in doing so, how simple is that? whether you watch the selections run or not is entirely up to you, the act of doing so generally leads to chasing losses especially if the method is having a bad day or days, but once your bets are placed that's the job done. If you are weak in nature then place the bets all at once in the morning and not race to race, then check the results the following day. Try to eliminate any form of tinkering with the method.

Note that all methods have losing runs and winning runs, fortunately both methods find winners almost every day, especially the One horse book method as a lot of these selections tend to be short in the betting. The Top mark method has a strike rate of about 30% so only 30 selections in 100 are going to win but as I have stated this method does find regular winners with no really long losing runs to date but with any form of betting expect the unexpected. I recently told someone who had signed up on my site to get these selections to keep the faith. In other words take everything the method throws at you, keep your head down and take the rough with the smooth. As I write the last selections of this particular day has just gone in at 13/2 BOG price 5/1 Starting price if this had not won I would have had a losing day. With racing now taking place seven days a week we know there is another challenge waiting tomorrow and the day after and the day after that!!

I believe in this method 100% and have not only been making money but banking money since the day I started using it. Yes I am having losing runs but taking great pleasure from the winning periods and I am in this for long term gains, as I stated keep the faith and long terms gains will be yours too. If you become a winning punter, which you will in the long term if you use this method correctly, your bookmaker will start to limit your bets or even ban you from their site. You may have to switch accounts to an exchange such as betfair to continue using this method. When you become successful, spend the profits you make and enjoy the money you make, that's what gambling is all about or why bother in the first place?

RESULTS TO DATE

Please note that updated results can be found on my website at

www.bettingsystem.info

Date	Selection	W/L	Totals
18/3	**Shut the Box W13/8**, Holly Bush Henry, **Savello W5/2**, Larkbarrow Lad **W15/8**, **Eyes Right W11/8**	+639	+40560
17/3	Jepeck	-100	+39921
16/3	Ashutor, Brother Tedd, **Paper Promise W15/8**, **Newberry New W11/4**, **Sams Adventure W2/1**, **Casual Cavalier W100/30**, Corinto, **Cap Horner** 13/2, The Cannister Man, **The Captains Inn W6/4**, Phosphor	+1393	+40021
15/3	Monsieur Lecoq, Cheerfilly, **Unforgiving Minute 11/8**, National Glory	-163	+38628
14/3	**Paisley Park W7/4**, Isabeg Lane, Sense of Direction, Galileo's Spear	-125	+38791
13/3	**Finawn Bawn W1/2**, Bbold, Apex King, **Camachess W11/10**, Ulster **Lothario W4/1**	+260	+38916
12/3	Exalted Angel, Bazarov, **Ragnar W3/1, Camachess W13/8, Pass the Vino W11/2**	+813	+38656
11/3	**Cadeaux Du Bresil W3/1**, SHamtung	+200	+37843
9/3	Dahawi, Whitehotchillifili, Derrianna Spirit, **Treacherous W4/1**	+100	+37643
8/3	Got Away, **Warrior's Valley W10/11**, Air Force Army, Rock on Rocky, **Decision Maker W7/2**	+141	+37543
7/3	Quite by Chance, Vis A Vis, **Green Dolphin W3/1**, Prince Dundee, **Christmas In Usa W6/5**, Road to Riches, Cappananty Con, **Frisella W4/7**	-29	+37402
6/3	Perfect Moment, Mortens Leam, **Iwilldoit W13/8, I'm Available W6/1**, Don Jupp, **Jahbath W1/1**	+563	+37431
5/3	**Smarty Wild W9/4**, Juge Et Parti, Decoration of War	+25	+36868
4/3	Valseur Du Granval, **Stonebrigg Legend W3/1**, Wanaasah	+100	+36843
3/3	Castletown, Stoney Stream, Stonemadforspeed, Fuseau	-400	+36743
2/3	Pogue, **Alizee De Janeiro W3/1**, Smiley Bagel, Danse Idol, Equus Amadeus	-100	+37143
1/3	Lacan, **Zmhar 4/7, Moonlight Spirit W1/4**, Coole Well, **The White Mouse W11/10**, Eddiemaurice	-108	+37243
28/2	**Kayf Blanco W2/1**, Uhlan Bute, Gold Chain, The Cannister Man, Passam Here's Herbie, **Old Salt W5/2, Alright Sunshine W5/4, Forest of Dean W11/8**, Ventura Blues, Invincible One, **Blazon W6/4**	+163	+37351
27/2	Champagne Mystery, Ostuni, Vanderbilt, **John Williams 8/11**, Solway Lark, Pot Luck	-427	+37188
26/2	**Trapper Peak W5/1, Al Kherb W4/1**, Fifty Shades, All Is Good, Cranbrook Causeway, Khage, **King RolandW8/13, Bay of Naples W5/6**	+645	+37615

Date	Selection	W/L	Totals
25/2	**Western Honour W11/10**, Rio Quinto, **Graystown W5/1**, Graasten, The Flying Sofa, Ormskirk, **Coopers Square W5/2**, The Cashel Man, **With Caution W8/11**	+433	+36970
24/2	If the Cap Fits, **Shantou Flyer 8/11**	-27	+36537
23/2	**Cool Mix W4/6**, Katgary, **Petite Jack W9/1**, Mr Scaramanga, **Samburu Shuja W11/4**, Overtown Express, Modeligo, **Alkaamel W8/11**	+915	+36564
22/2	**Epatante W1/5, Reve W4/7**, Straidnahanna, Hey Bill, Top Power, Jack the Truth	-323	+35649
21/2	**Ingleby Hollow W10/11**, Mistercobar, **I'm To Blame W8/11, Clondaw Castle W10/11**, Black Salt, Destinys Rock, Dark Allaliance, Plumette	-245	+35972
20/2	Grand Inquisitor, Champagne Well, **Black Buble W7/1, Desert Ruler 9/2**, Red Loopy, Annie For, **Doctor Dex W13/8**, Sir Mangan, Murdanova, **Lucky Deal W7/4**, Zorawar	+788	+36217
18/2	Shroughmore Lass, **Full Throttle W11/10, Dorking Cock W4/5**, Kingdom of Dubai	-10	+35429
17/2	Ivilnoble, Supakalanistic, Longhousesignora	-300	+35439
16/2	Yanworth, **Road to Rome W13/8**, Sceau Royal,Something Lucky, Grey Brittain, Caspar The Cub	-338	+35739
15/2	Sir Egbert, Kalashnikov, Elusive Belle, **Achille W9/2, Copperhead W9/4 Pistol Whipped W13/8, Kayf Blanco W4/1**, Florencio, Elysees Palace, Native Fighter, **Lion Hearted W10/11, Orchid Star W1/7** Lord of The Glen	+643	+36077
14/2	**Dream Du Grand Val W4/7, We Have A Dream W2/5**, Definitely Red, Inch Lala, **Hurricane Dylan 15/8**, Bullfrog	-15	+35434
13/2	**Acey Milan W11/8**, Et Moi Alors, Poperinghe Ginger, Qawamees, **Purple Rock W3/1**, Addicted to You	+38	+35449
6/2	Chambard, Diomede Des Mottes, Picture Poet, Imperial Prince, **Zorawar W5/4**	-275	+35411
5/2	Bachelor	-100	+35686
3/2	Southfield Stone, **Dunhallow Gesture 8/11, Solar Park 1/4, Marhaban 1/2**	+48	+35786
2/2	**Orchid Star W2/9**, Come on Tier, Inaam, **Galitello W5/1**, Enzemble	+222	+35738
31/1	Alcanar, Eve Harrington	-200	+35516
30/1	Bobby Biscuit, Simple Thought, Gravity Wave, Mac O'polo	-400	+35716
29/1	**Nestor Park W13/8**	+163	+36116
28/1	Extra Mag, Talkischeap, **Pym W8/13, Supakalanistic W7/2**	+216	+35953
27/1	Whiteoak Fleur, Bredon Hill Lad, Urbanist	-300	+35737

Date	Selection	W/L	Totals
26/1	Theo's Charm, **Fearsome W1/1,** Nonesuch, **Nubough 4/9** **Joegogo W3/1**	+244	+36037
25/1	**Scarlet Dragon W2/1**, Ermyn's Emerald, Magic of Light, Maroc, Antonia Clara	-200	+35793
23/1	**St Peters Basilica W1/1,** Vandella, Kamra	-100	+35993
22/1	**Clondaw Castle W6/4,** Working Class	+50	+36093
21/1	**Ingleby Hollow 15/8,** Beallandendall, **Windsor Avenue W10/11, Emerald Chieftain W4/1**	+579	+36043
20/1	Galactic Power, **Ask Ben W10/11, Destrier W4/5**	+71	+35464
19/1	Un Prophete, Boite, Redicean, **Probability W6/5, Wakanda W15/2** Sylva Eclipse, Designated	+370	+35393
18/1	High Acclaim, **Lisnagar Oscar W9/4, Samburu Shujaa W4/1**, Smaoineamh Alainn, Rock Bottom, Given Choice	+225	+35023
17/1	Humble Hero, Perfect Predator, Iwilldoit, Rockcliffe, **Cracking Destiny W2/1**, Landing Night, Steelriver	-400	+34798
16/1	Harambe, Maratt, Three Star General, **Debestyman W2/1**, Woods, Clovelly Bay	-300	+35198
15/1	Kalaskadesemilley, **Ulster W11/4,** Tamerlane	+75	+35498
14/1	**Whatswrongwithyou W4/7**, Misty Mai, Umndeni, Mortens Leam, Mount Ararat	-343	+35423
13/1	Barossa Red, Lord Yeats, **Martila W2/1**, Eureu Du Boulay	-100	+35766
12/1	Minnies Secret, **Manwell 10/11, Tough Remedy 6/4**	+141	+35866
11/1	Bug Boy, Philamundo, Ventura Blues, Precious Bounty, **Dell Oro W2/1** Nortonthorpelegend, **Rock Bottom W9/4**	-75	+35725
10/1	**Uno Mas W5/4, Flowery W7/2, Jimmy Rabbitte W2/5,** Midnight Malibu **Three Weeks W5/4,** Black Salt, Mad Jack Mytton, **Brecon Hill W1/1**	+440	+35800
9/1	Secret Ace, **Court House W8/11,** Aguerooo, **Diamond Gait W11/10,** Fox Appeal, Cenotaph	-217	+35360
8/1	**Two for Gold W10/11,** Frenchy Du Large, **Ribble Valley 5/4**	+116	+35577
7/1	**Ontopoftheword W2/5, Wot A Shot W4/1,** Rainy City, **Alright Sunshine W4/6,** Sevarano, **Top and Drop W4/1, Dashel Drasher W13/8, Given Choice W11/10**, Zoraya	+885	+35461
6/1	Kheros, Oden	-200	+34576
5/1	**Torpillo W1/3, Laurina W1/7, Kapcorse W2/5**, Perseid, Harvey Dent	-113	+34776
4/1	One Handsome Dude, Dalkadam, Bastien, The Knot Is Tied, **Clarendon Street W2/5**, Demophon, Skydiving, Freedom and Wheat	-660	+34889
3/1	**Capone 8/11**, Great Tempo, Ruler of The Nile, **Weld Al Emarat W15/8** Steal the Scene	-39	+35549
2/1	Las Tunas, Present Flight, **Liberty Bella W4/1**, Royal Prospect	+100	+35588
1/1	Al Kherb, Always Lion, Some Chaos, Flight to Milan, Stonebrigg Legend, Foxtrot Juliet	-600	+35488
31/12	Gin Palace, Printing Dollars, Pine Warbler, **Burrows Park 5/1**	+200	+36088
30/12	Dark Magic, Shiroccan Roll, Percy Street, Ice Cool Champs	-400	+35888
29/12	**Mighty Thunder W9/2,** Tokaramore, Majestic Moon, Di's Gift, **I'm A Game Changer W15/2**	+900	+36288

Date	Selection	W/L	Totals
28/12	Lady Cosette, **Let Rip W5/4**, Odds on Oli, **Arthur Mac W2/1**, **Nortonthorpelegend W15/2**, Boruma	+775	+35388
27/12	Kingsplace, Top Gamble, Imperial Acolyt, **Flegmatic W6/5**, Galileo's Spear **Princess Salaman W9/4, Altior W1/5**	-35	+34613
26/12	Schiehallion Munro, **Eureu Du Boulay W11/4, Posh Trish 2/5**, **Paddleyourowncanoe 9/1, Flic Ou Voyou 11/4**, Sir Egbert, **Chivers W10/11**, Shininstar	+1281	+34648
22/12	Bingo D'Olivate, Becker, Almost Gold, **Ballymoy 11/8**, Theo's Charm	-262	+33367
21/12	Holiday Magic, Deebaj, The Boss's Dream, **Vindication W4/6**	-233	+33629
20/12	Country 'n' Western, Shalakar, Goodgirlteresa, Turtle Cask	-400	+33862
19/12	Dove Divine, Great Shout, Nordic Combined, Drinks Interval, **Capeland W9/4**, Sir Ottoman	-220	+34262
18/12	Young Phoenix	-100	+34482
17/12	Chivers, Fast Track, Lady Lizzie, **Anycity W3/1**	Level	+34582
16/12	**Earlofthecotswolds W4/7**, Xpo Universal, **Isaacstown Lad W6/1**, Rosie And Millie	+457	+34582
15/12	Newtown Boy, Robbing the Prey, **Quel Destiny W10/11, O O Seven W6/4**, Top and Drop, **Coeur Blimey W7/1**, Late Shipment, **Persian Sun W11/10, Brain Power W7/1, El Hombre W9/2**	+1800	+34125
14/12	**Same Circus W11/2**, Smaoineamh Alainn, Amazing Comedy, **Golden Jeffrey W13/8**, Sir Mangan, Pipes of Peace	+313	+32325
13/12	**Southfield Stone W30/100**, Jester Jet, Black Buble, Church Hall, Edwardstone, Eye of The Water	-470	+32012
12/12	Kapga De Lily, **Ebony Gal W6/4**, Dyliev, She Mite Bite, **Mainsail Athletic W6/4**, Ask the Tycoon, Just the Man, More Than More, Wimpole Hall	-400	+32482
11/11	**Stop Talking W5/4, Antunes W6/5**, Micquus, **The Ogle Gogle Man W11/10**	+255	+32882
10/11	**Wolfcatcher W6/5**, Tzar De L'elfe, Regal Banner	-80	+32627
9/12	Thomas Campbell	-100	+32707
7/12	**Millie The Minx W7/4, Ninepointsixthree W6/1, Gonnabegood W4/1**, Remastered, Eamon an Cnoic, **Carnival Queen W10/11, Debonair 7/2**	+1416	+32807
6/12	Foundation Man, Rocku, **Glory of Paris W2/1**, Firmament	-100	+31391
5/12	Wirral Girl, **Shininstar W13/2, Newtide W7/4, Absolute Dylan W11/4**, Al Messila, Whinging	+800	+31491
4/12	Soaring Spirits, Tomily, Madame Vitesse, Bang Bang Rosie, Ring Minella	-500	+30691
3/12	Life Knowledge, Pride's Gold	-200	+31191
2/12	Navajo War Dance, Barrys Jack, **Kings Eclipse W8/1**	+600	+31391
1/12	Burrenbridge Hotel, **Shantaluze W9/4**, Sunnyahliateigan, Lorna Cole	-75	+30791
29/11	Some Day Soon, Definate Winner, **Unblinking W13/8, Manorah W2/1**, Hello Bangkok, Valley Belle, Glory of Paris, True Destiny	-238	+30866
28/11	Agincourt Reef, The Boss's Dream, **Always Resolute 100/30**, Roland Rocks	+33	+31104
27/11	Et Moi Alors, Ar Mast, Moonlight Dancer, Coiste Bodhar, Torrid	-500	+31071

Date	Selection	W/L	Totals
26/11	Forsee, The Ogle Gogle Man, All Hail Caesar	-300	+31571
25/11	Shintori	-100	+31871
24/11	Stoney Mountain, **If the Cap Fits 8/11**, Very First Time, Dellusionsofgrandeur, Briyouni, Just Glamorous, Boagrius	-527	+31971
23/11	Sutters Mill, Gone Platinum, **Wenyourreadyfreddie W4/6, Moonlighter W100/30**, Flying Angel, Braavos, **Inhale W7/4**	+172	+32478
22/11	Dandolo Du Gite, Cottonvale, Eragon De Chanay, Victoria Drummond, **Cantiniere W10/11**	-310	+32306
20/11	Hill sixteen, Blottos, Teescomponents Lad, Mac Cennetig, **Le Frank W7/2, My Mate Mark W9/4**, Biddy the Boss, Spirit of Zebedee, **Earl of Bunnacurry W5/4**, Glorious Emaraty, Robert L'Echelle, **Watersmeet W11/4**	+175	+32616
19/11	Bermeo, **Diocles Of Rome W15/8**	+88	+32441
18/11	**Silver Sea W9/2**, Moabit, Waltz, The Lincoln Lawyer, Morney Wing, Arquebusier, Dynamite Dollar	-150	+32353
17/11	**Barys W3/1**, Skidoosh, **Miles to Milan W6/4**, Becky The Thatcher, Ravens Tower, One of Us, Vincente	-50	+32503
16/11	Uncle Jerry, **Wohileh W3/1**, Lucymai, Copal	Level	+32553
15/11	Georgina Joy, Mr Lando, Sadma, Annie Bonny, The Happy Chappy, Jennys Day, Momentarily	-700	+32553
14/11	Clingerside, Anytime Now, Al Destoor, **Casual Cavalier W100/30**, Steps and Stairs, **Maria's Benefit W4/7**, Orchard Thieves	-113	+33253
13/11	Space Oddity, **Remember Forever W6/1**, Hogan's Height	+400	+33366
12/11	Ey Up Rocky, Lexington Law, Trooblue, Dolos	-400	+32966
11/11	Kings Walk, Steele Native	-200	+33366
10/11	Tangled, **Donjuan Triumphant 3/1**, Buster Thomas, **Bags Groove 5/4** Romain De Senam, Burrenbridge Hotel, **Sojourn 9/4**	+250	+33566
9/11	**Elysees W4/5, Windsor Avenue W1/3, Weather Front W11/10**, Molly Childers, Sounds of Italy, **Alright Jack W3/1**	+323	+33316
8/11	The Ogle Gogle Man, **Informateur W4/7**, Posh Trish, Ready to Rumble the Jugopolist 20/1	-343	+32993
7/11	**Surfman W4/5**, Private Secretary, Hawaam, Son of Feyan, Good Boy Alfie Golden Jeffrey, Settimo Milanses, Balibour, Balleticon, Executive Force	-820	+33336
6/11	**Leodis Dream W4/5**, Power Home, Some Day Soon, Lucky Lodge **Nivaldo W13/8**	-45	+34156
5/11	Hopes Wishes, Milldean Star, **Salute the Soldier W1/1**	-100	+34201
4/11	Cyrname	-100	+34301
3/11	Pym, Art Mauresque, Smugglers Creek	-300	+34401
2/11	Knight Commander, Queens Magic, No Hiding Place, Dawnieriver **Graceful Lady W9/4**, Denmead	-275	+34701
1/11	Cillians Well, **Champagne to Go W100/30**, Pennsylvania Dutch	+130	+34976
31/10	Starjac, Movewiththetimes	-200	+34846
30/10	**Anytime Will Do W5/4**, Boy in A Bentley, Doctor Dex, Kings Highway	-175	+35046

Date	Selection	W/L	Totals
29/10	Quri, **Scheu Time W1/6**, Vincent's Forever	-183	+35221
28/10	**Cahill W3/1**	+300	+35404
27/10	**Young Rascal DH5/4, King Golan W6/1, Middlebrow W9/4, Dinons W10/11, Strong Glance 6/1**	+1579	+35104
26/10	Franz Kafka, Court Minstrel, Bang on Frankie, Verve	-400	+33525
25/10	Stowaway Magic, Cause Toujours, Ballymilan, Zabeel Star, Agamemmon Minella Fiveo, Royal Ruby, **New Agenda W15/2**	+50	+33925
24/10	Psychoandy, Rapper, Jarlath, High Command, **Morney Wing W3/1,** Summer Moon, Safrani, **Hard Toffee W4/1**	+100	+33875
23/10	Maqsad, **Nashirah W6/5**, Cadeau Magnifique, Gorham's Cave	-180	+33775
22/10	Dream Machine, **Fresh Terms W9/4**, Crownthorpe, Seventi, Call to Order Between the Waters, Gifts of Gold, Blue Mountain	-475	+33955
21/10	**Verdana Blue 5/6,** Baron Du Plessis, Boric	-117	+34430
20/10	**Ice Gala W4/9, Dandolo Du Gite 10/11,** Clock on Tom, Etamine Du Cochet, Khanisari, Highway to One, Master Dee, Sheriff Garrett	-465	+34547
19/10	Elieden, Barys, Bardd, **Move Legend W4/1,** Izzer, **Boston George W6/4**	+150	+35012
18/10	Quids In, Shamshon, Itizzit, **Karnavaal W7/4**, Muneyra	-225	+34862
17/10	Deebee 11/8, **Chitra W3/1**	+200	+35087
16/10	**Muntadab W9/2, What's Occurring W5/2**	+700	+34887
15/10	Tarboosh, **Jahbath W8/11**	-27	+34187
14/10	**Jam Session W3/1**, Noble Peace, Coolanly, I'm A Game Changer	Level	+34214
13/10	**Persian King W5/4**, Monbeg Legend, Sneaky Feeling, Rock the Kasbah, **Jonah Jones W15/8**, Baydar, Master Carpenter, El Gumryah	-288	+34214
12/10	Flying Tiger, Midnight Glory, Pretty Pollyanna, Surya, Intrepidly	-500	+34502
11/10	**Awake at Midnight W11/10, Royal Ruby W7/2,** Never A Word	+360	+35002
10/10	**McGroarty W5/4**, Bristol Missile, **Sovereign Grant W15/8**, Elector	+113	+34642
9/10	Prestbury Park	-100	+34529
8/10	Sam Red, **Lungarno Palace W13/8**, Gloweth, Isomer	-138	+34629
7/10	Vaniteux, Romulus Du Donjon	-200	+34767
6/10	Ventura Ocean, Our Three Sons, Brown Bear, **Turgenev W7/4, Klassique W4/1,** Cape Byron, Holmeswood	+75	+34967
5/10	Sixties Secret, **Jaunty Thor W10/11**, Great Beyond	-110	+34892
4/10	Noble Peace, Krystallite, **Hepijeu W9/4**	+25	+35002
3/10	**Clara Peters W9/2**, Chynna 2/1, Louie De Palma, **Wandrin StarW 3/1**	+550	+34977
2/10	Caid Du Lin, Brave Spartacus, Panko, **Daawy W6/4**, Donnelly's Rainbow	-250	+34427
1/10	**Green or Black 9/4, On Demand 6/4,** Valhalla	+275	+34677

Date	Selection	W/L	Totals
30/9	**Nate The Great W1/5**	+20	+34402
29/9	Guroor, Arthur Kitt, **Barristan The Bold W9/4**, African Ride Wohileh	-175	+34382
28/9	Unforgetable Filly, Main Edition, **Wise Council W4/7**, Elegiac	-243	+34558
27/9	Make A Wish, **Global Jackpot W4/5**, Amilliontimes, Cockley Beck, Drill, Buffalo River, **San Donato W1/1**, Elector	-420	+34801
26/9	London Protocol, **Master Carpenter W7/2, Make My Heart Fly W1/1**	+350	+35221
25/9	**Sameem 11/4, Detachment W11/10**, Welsh Lord, Silk Run, Handmaiden	+85	+34871
24/9	Happy Power, **Faro Angel W5/6**, Forest View, Taurean Dancer, **Turgenev 4/6**, Smashing Lass	-250	+34786
23/9	**Handy Hollow W9/2**, Seduce Me	+350	+35036
22/9	**Anasheed 6/5, Swordbill 5/4**, Di Alta, Shouranour, Shumookhi	-55	+34686
21/9	Quite by Chance, Scoop the Pot, **Dirty Rascal W11/10**, Beat Le Bon	-190	+34741
20/9	Dark Jedi, Silvery Moon, Buonarroti, Sky Patrol, Boerham, Pioneering, **Baritone 1/2**	-550	+34931
19/9	Aquanura, Sovereign Grant, **Encore D'Or W11/8**, Tricky Dicky, Forever Field	-263	+35481
18/9	Harpelle, **Romola 2/1**, Hint of Grey, Heavenly Guest	-100	+35744
17/9	**Bermeo W4/1, Stacey Sue W1/1, Baltic Prince W7/2, Kamikaze Lord W4/6**, Cuban Heel	+817	+35844
15/9	Daphinia, Dakota Gold, Oh This Is Us, Night of Glory, Spray the Sea Lynwood Gold, **Voluminous W7/2**, Orange Suit	-350	+35027
14/9	**Swift and Sure W6/5**	+120	+35377
13/9	The Irish Rover, Fox Fearless, Nuns Walk, Tolkyn	-400	+35257
12/9	**Mr Caffrey W9/4**, Val Mome, Inexes, Smart Illusion, **Quicksand W1/1**	+25	+35657
11/9	Good Tyne Girl	-100	+35632
9/9	Nordican Bleue, Code of Law, Desiremoi D'Authie	-300	+35732
8/9	Tommy Taylor, **Innocent Touch W9/4**, McCabe Creek, **Rene Mathis 9/4**	+250	+36032
7/9	Gallic, Bangkok, **Sky Defender W10/11**, Mainsail Atlantic, Alfurat River, Its All A Joke	-409	+35782
6/9	Wicked Sea, **Peppay Le Pugh W8/11**, Apterix, Volcanic Sky	-227	+36191
5/9	Canavese, Babyfact, Pimilico Pleaser, **Beat That W2/7, Discay W17/2 The Jam Man W13/8, Angel of Harlem W4/5**, Silver Crescent	+722	+36418
4/9	**Henry Smith W4/7**, Agreement, **Mr Caffrey W15/8, Line of Duty W2/1 Soldier in Action W11/4**, Cogital, Peggy Sue, **Psychotic W9/2, Goodwood Showman 3/1**	+1170	+35696
3/9	Islay Mist, **Dirty Rascal W10/11, Hard Taskmaster W5/6**, Prabeni	-26	+34526
2/9	**All Set to Go W7/2**, Archie	+250	+34552
1/9	**Leapaway W1/3**, Top Chief, Lualiwa, Bertog, The Third Man, Liamba, Leroy Leroy	-567	+34202

Date	Selection	W/L	Totals
31/8	Grey Galleon, Narjes, **Captain Peacock W1/1**, Who's De Baby, **Kingston W9/2, Muthhila W6/5**, Theatre of War, Guardia **Svizzera W11/10**, Groundworker	+180	+34769
30/8	Federal Law, Blackheath, Beautiful People, Old Salt	-400	+34589
29/8	Valentino Sunrise, **Romaana W1/3, Maaward W5/4, Jedhi W7/4**	+233	+34989
28/8	Dolcissimo, Regulation	-200	+34756
27/8	**Indian Viceroy W1/2, Zorro W13/2,** Five Amarones, **Ormesher 11/8,** Kilfinichen Kitchen	+638	+34956
26/8	Sussex Girl, The Big Bad	-200	+34318
25/8	**Emerald Approach W 1/1**, Look Around, The Steward, **Nayef Road W11/10, Expert Eye 5/4**, Island Song	+60	+34518
24/8	Momkin, **Stradivarius 4/11**, Nate The Great	-264	+34458
23/8	Hilight, Firmament, **Lah Ti Dar W1/1**, Aquirer, Rawdaa, **Longhouse Sale 2/5**	-260	+34722
22/8	Impart, Lucky Beggar, Rickyroadboy, Natural Scenery, **Psychedelic Rock W7/2**	-50	+34982
21/8	Union Rose, **Enzemble W7/4, Fennaan W7/2, Cleni Wells, Choco Box W 1/1,** Viscount Loftus	+425	+35032
20/8	**Topical 11/10**, Atlantic Storm, Petrastar	-90	+34607
19/8	Lynwood Gold, Gustav Mahler	-200	+34697
18/8	Good Fortune, **Missy Mischief W13/8, Caius Marcus W4/1,** Amilliontimes, **Saunter W7/2**, Cool Macavity	+613	+34897
17/8	With A Start, **Lovin W6/4**, Cat Royale, **Little Jo W9/4**	+175	+34284
16/8	**Glass Slippers W5/4, Archie Perkins W9/4**, Calendimaggio, Courtside, Buxted Dream	+50	+34109
15/8	Marettimo, **Cracker Factory W1/5**, Kingson, Blue Reflection, **Signore Piccolo W100/30, Chain of Daisies W9/4, Outrageous Romana W9/2** Desirable Court, Mr Caffrey, Cotton Club, **Jumeirah Street W5/2**	+345	+34059
14/8	Cowboy Soldier, Sootability	-200	+33714
13/8	Three Saints Bay, **Central City W5/4, Penarth Pier W9/4, It's the Only Way W4/7**	+307	+33914
12/8	**Rotherhithe W10/11**, Recollect, **Perfect Symphony W4/1**, Simpson **W4/1,** Vimy Ridge	+691	+33607
11/8	Toffee Galore, **Forward Thinker W9/2**, Absolute Dream, **Royal Regent W13/2, Slipstream W5/2**	+1150	+32916
10/8	Desert Lantern	-100	+31766
9/8	King Crimson, Glenn Coco, Muttawaffer, **Belle Meade W100/30**	+33	+31866
8/8	Final Rock**, Ventura Ocean W11/8**, Shouranour, Reverend Jacobs, First Flight, Following Breeze, Sussex Girl, Trouble and Strife, **Laith Alereen 5/4 Letmestopyouthere W5/6,** Zaajer	-355	+31833
7/8	Al Mortajaz, Explain	-200	+32188
6/8	Angels, **Chantecler 13/2**	+550	+32388
5/8	Ezanak, Ravished, **Longhouse Sale 1/4, The Trader 11/10**, Rockin Boy	-165	+31838

Date	Selection	W/L	Totals
4/8	Major Partneship W2/7, New Jazz, Mistress Quickly, Margub W4/7 Branscombe W4/1, Top Score, Tarboosh W9/4	+411	+32003
3/8	Mr Caffrey, Get Ready Freddy, Donny Belle, Mankib W6/4, Island of Life Haadhir, Dolcissimo, Jacks Point, Our Charlie Brown	-650	+31592
2/8	Royal Plaza W4/7, Alexander the Grey, Drumhart, James Street W7/4, Lady Cosette, Isaan Queen, Zalshah W5/1, Top Break, Private Cashier Argito W6/5	+242	+32242
1/8	Ink Master W4/1, Angel's Envy, Rathobone, Poets Dawn, Abushamah Dark Shadow W15/8, Artarmon W7/2, Takiah	+438	+32000
31/7	Youghal By the Sea W5/6, Theydon Park	-17	+31562
30/7	Mullarkey, Twister, Tripartite, Wavepoint 100/30	+33	+31579
29/7	Solar Gold, Imperial Presence W5/2	+150	+31546
28/7	Gabriel The Wire, Baronial Pride, Staycation, Star of The EastW 5/4	-175	+31396
27/7	Sonic W7/4, Mr Caffrey, Ascended, Princess Power W4/1, Beshaayir, I'lletyougonow, Timoshenko W8/11, Fairlight W8/11	+320	+31571
26/7	La Pelosa, The Last but One W5/6, Tidal Watch, Little Windmill W10/1, Arabian Jazz, Gripper, Dive for Gold, Ragstone View, Abel Talisman, Vision Clear, Right Direction W10/11	+374	+31251
25/7	Bayshore Freeway W4/5, Rastacap, Solesmes W15/8, Heartwarming W2/5, Clenymistra	+108	+30877
24/7	Instant Attraction, Advanced Hero W8/13, Gang Warfare, Ellen Gates 9/4, Mayassar W8/13, Piece of History 11/8, Sanam	+186	+30769
23/7	Axe Axelrod, Queen Jo Jo 8/11	-27	+30583
22/7	Cotton Club, Ornua W4/6, Leapaway W1/3, Grey Spirit W11/10 Orions Bow	+10	+30610
21/7	Fact of The Matter, Damiens Dilemma, Wise Council, Lake Volta, Major Partnership W8/13, Deep Sea, Line of Duty	-538	+30600
20/7	Loch Ness Monster W4/7, Improvising, Summerghand W4/1, Miss Latin, Travel Lightly, Showout W1/3, Ventura Knight, Hot Team	-10	+31138
19/7	Straighttothepoint, Rockin Boy 4/7, Moxy Mares, Silca Mistress, Mutadel Carries Vision, Stifonic, Sister Celine, Sha La La Lee	-743	+31148
18/7	Deia Glory W1/1, Penny Dreadful, Thoughtfully, Persian Moon W11/8 Chetan, Spring Romance, Silver Character	-263	+31891
17/7	Foxy Boy, Altra Vita, Island Song W6/4, Scoop the Pot, Passing Call W1/1, Penwood, Arabian Jazz	-250	+32154
16/7	Kilbarchan, Sultan Baybars, Pipers Note W11/4, Magical Wish W1/1	+175	+32404
15/7	Jassas, Old Salt, Deadly Move	-300	+32229
14/7	Dal Harraild, Mill Green W1/4, Southfield Theatre, Duke of Hazard, Bedouin's Story W10/11, Ferrier, Woodside Wonder 1/1	-184	+32529
13/7	Dirty Rascal W13/8, Semoun W6/5, Could It Be Love, Alpha Centauri W4/9, Trafalgar Rock, Joueur Bresilien W2/1, Barkis, Court Duty	+127	+32713
12/7	Wells Farhh Go W15/2, Emaraaty, Why We Dream W5/2, Dapper Man, Hafeet Alain W11/1, Affina, Iconic Knight, Supernova W4/5, Arcadian Angel, Fox Coach, Berkshire Spirit, Dangerous Ends, Highland Acclaim W13/2	+1930	+32586
11/7	Good Impression, Trouble and Strife W5/6, Pink Iceburg W1/1, Shyjack Watheeqa W1/3	+16	+30656
10/7	Danehill Desert, Herculean W2/5, Ifandbutwhynot W5/1, G for Ginger W3/1, Genetics W5/4, Bombshell Bay W2/1	+1065	+30640

Date	Selection	W/L	Totals
9/7	Master Sunrise, **Weightfordave W5/6**, Balkinstown, **Vallarta W7/2**, Sotomayor	+133	+29575
8/7	Corton Lad	-100	+29442
7/7	**Thriving W5/6, Fashion Theory W6/1**, Makambe, On A May Day	+483	+29542
6/7	Ocelot, Rainbow, **Betty F W9/4, Mr Mafia W7/4, Mustashry W11/4, Cupboard Love W4/1**, Greaves, La Figlia W2/1	+975	+29059
5/7	Stay in Touch, Mitcd, **Jonah Jones W5/4**, Pablo Escobar,**Tapis Libre W7/2**, Fair Power, Chai Chai	-25	+28084
4/7	Light Hearted, Zeshov, Balgapar, **Skin Deep W8/11**, Dr Dunraven, Orions Bow, Manfullet, **Vale of Kent W6/5, Altra VitaW 8/11, Groveman W8/11**, Petitioner, Chloellie	+462	+28109
3/7	Knight in Armour, **Brexit Time W11/8, The Great Wall W11/8, Matchmaking W4/7**, Enzo, Glanvilles Guest	+32	+28571
2/7	**Construct W10/11,** X Rated 7/2, **I Believe You W11/8**, Corton Lad, Never Surrender	-72	+28539
1/7	**Celestial Path W6/4, Fair Mountain W4/9, Leapaway 9/4**, Perseid, **Argentello 4/9**	+363	+28611
30/6	Come on Lester, Kabrit, Dragons Tail, Dynamic, Noble Star	-500	+28248
29/6	**Blonde Warrior 2/5**, Arabian Gift, **Souriyan 11/4**	+215	+28748
28/6	Hyanna, Roll on Rory, Plant of Power, Classic Pursuit, Ravenhoe, Highland Pass, Royal Cosmic, **Desert Fire W10/11**	-609	+28533
27/6	**Forseti W2/1**, Kasbah, **Okool W6/4, Thimbleweed W5/4**, Spoilt Rotten, Fort Gabriel, Massini's Dream, **Kalagia W7/4**, Sporting Chance, Poyle Charlotte	+50	+29142
26/6	**Victory Command W1/10**, Oriental Splendour, **On A May Day W 1/3, Outofthequestion W9/4**, Lolita Pulido, Mogestic	-41	+29092
25/6	**Lotus Pond W4/9, Timeforwest W7/2**, Free Stone Hill, David's Phobebe, Craigmor, Glamorous Dream, **Kaanoon W7/4**	+169	+29133
24/6	Hazarfiya, Zubayr	-200	+28964
23/6	**Byrons Choice W5/1**, Natalie's Joy, **Crystal Ocean 4/7**, Icefall, Tanarpino, Golden Jeffrey, **Port Douglas 11/4**	+532	+29164
21/6	Revich, **Shailene W4/6**, Cupboard Love, Blue Havana, **Big Time Maybe W4/9**	-189	+28632
20/6	Sense of Belonging, Dontgiveuponbob, Twojayslad, Lucymai, Roman River, Multellie	-600	+28821
19/6	Stylish Dancer, **Crageelagh Girl W4/5**, Morando, Sea Youmzain, Roddy	-320	+29421
18/6	**Society Queen W4/6**, Arabian Jazz, Implicit, Wolf Hunter	-233	+29741
17/6	White Light, **Gumriyah W10/11**	-10	+29974
16/6	Indian Voyage, Swift and Sure, Mr Fickle, Guerrilla Tactics, Generous Chief, **Chaleur 4/6**, Beyond Equal	-533	+29984
15/6	**Settie Hill W4/6,** Passing Call, Eagle Hunter, Daybreak, Weinberg	-333	+30517
14/6	**Sea of Class W2/5**, Muscika, Giving Glances, Mashaheer, Patrick, **Escobar W100/30, L'Inganno Felice W4/7, Holryale W13/8**	+190	+30850
13/6	**Caliburn W5/4, Sofia's Rock W8/1**, Kraka, **Red Island W6/4, Courtside W13/8, Drill W9/2**, Suzi's Connoisseur, **Airshow W4/1, Cameo Star DH 4/1**, Afandem	+1988	+30660

Date	Selection	W/L	Totals
12/6	Pilot Wings, Rebel State, **Mutafani W4/11**, Crimean Queen, **Howman W11/8**, Hidden Steps, King Calypso, **The Devils Drop W4/5**, **Je Suis Charlie W11/10**	-137	+28672
11/6	Kilfinichen Bay, Eyehaveadoodidea, Dory	-300	+28809
10/6	Tarboosh	-100	+29109
9/6	Reverend Jacobs, **Sea Youmzain W9/4**, Last Page, Knowing Glance, Gaelic Flow	-175	+29209
8/6	Only Spoofing, Kensington Star, Recollect, Move Swiftly, Monsieur Gibraltar	-500	+29384
7/6	**Beachwalk W11/4**, **Blonde Warrior W4/9**, Mutafarrid, **Marylin W1/1 Soldiers Call W4/6**, Bashiba, **Savaanah W4/5**, Regal Mirage, Sharja Silk Zorovian	+166	+29884
6/6	**Excellent Team W5/2**, **Amirr W11/8**, Cayuga, Natalie Express, **Prides Gold W 5/4**, Sir Dancealot, **Aasheq W13/8**, **Cococabala W10/1**, Scottish Summit, Straight Ash, **Red Mist W8/11**	+1349	+29718
5/6	**Fair Mountain W2/1**, Our Three Sons, **Mogestic W7/2**, Stormbay Bomber, Awsome Rosie, Sword of Fate, Pouvoir Magique	+50	+28369
4/6	Ready Token, Fly the Nest	-200	+28319
3/6	**Indian Temple W3/1**, **Titus Bolt W4/1**, **Curious Carlos W11/8**, Martiloo **Master of Finance W7/2**, Bisboubisou, Millen Dollar Man	+888	+28519
2/6	Mac Cennetig, Makethedifference, Lincoln Rocks, Royal Brave, **Shaybani W4/5**	-320	+27631
1/6	**Eeh Bah Gum W1/1**, Mick Thonic, God Willing, Wafy	-300	+27951
31/5	Musical Art, **Gift of HeraW5/2**, Trump Alexander, Floral Bouquet Mesquite, Shailene	-250	+28251
30/5	**Weellan W3/1**, **Northwest Frontier W10/11**, Robinroyale	+291	+28501
29/5	Murqaab, **Catavina W3/1**, **Worth Waiting W8/11**, **Rickyroadboy W7/2** General Ginger, **Ledham W4/6**, Prying Pandora	+490	+28210
28/5	**The Last Party W13/8**	+163	+27720
27/5	**Code ff Law 10/1**, Kilmurvy, Kapstadt	+800	+27552
26/5	**Mirage Dancer W1/1**, Eastern Lady, Inaminna, **Embour W3/1**, Roser Moter	+100	+26752
25/5	Swiss Chime, Ynys Mon, **Deauville Crystal W10/1**	+800	+26652
24/5	Mr Bossy Boots, Innoko, **Mutawafer W5/4**, Herecomesthesun, King of Dreams **Poet's WordW 4/6**	-188	+25852
23/5	**Black Sam Bella W13/8**, Alf N Dor, **Lalania W9/2**, **Bailarico W6/4**, Slow to Hand, Titi Mafki, **Jawal W11/10**, The Warrior	+423	+26040
22/5	Popping Corks, Ausin Powers, Hatcher, **Inchcolm W15/2**	+450	+25617
21/5	Hard Forest, **Hermisita W11/8**, **The Tin Man 7/4**, Biotic	+113	+25167
20/5	Glorious Player, **Tigre Du Terre W1/4**, **Miss Adventure W4/6**, **Mr Mafia W8/1**, Destiny's Gold, Rapid Fritz, **Forgot to Ask W5/4**	+717	+25054
19/5	**Queen of Bermuda W4/6**, Magical Effect, **Purser W6/4**, Suzi's Connoissuer, Yellow Dockets, Between the Waters, **Get Ready Freddie W3/1**, **Victory Command W3/1**	+417	+24337

Date	Selection	W/L	Totals
18/5	**Al Muffrih W13/8**	+163	+23920
17/5	**My Escapade W4/1**, Coopers Friend, **I Am A Dreamer W8/1**, Zairah, Stamford Raffles	+900	+23757
16/5	Harry Angel 4/7, International Man, **Champ 1/7**, Shanaway, Volpone Jelois, Christmas Night	-329	+22857
15/5	**Deep Intrigue W4/5**, The Detainee, Ruby Russet, More Bucks, General Mahler, **Settie Hill 1/7**	-306	+23186
14/5	Lester Kris, Ballycamp, No No Juliet, Riddlestown	-400	+23492
5/5	Young Phoenix, Little Miss Poet, Humbert, **Pepita W7/2, Fujaira Prince W10/11**, Spirit of Zebedee, **Nyaleti W7/2**, Alrahaal, General Mahler, **Card Game W12/1**, Swashbuckle	+1291	+23892
4/5	Josiebond, Ravenswood, Wallflower	-300	+22601
3/5	**Robsdelight W7/4**, Poet's Princess, **Captain Lars W10/11**, Playfull Spirit, **Florencio W5/2**, Best Tamyuz, Reveleon, Puds, Northwest Frontier, **Seen The Lyte W6/4**	+66	+22901
2/5	The Irish Rover, **Invincible Army W6/4**, Accidental Agent, Balmoral Castle Azor Ahai, Making Miracles, Leeshaan, Princess Kiera, **Tin Hat W4/6**, Club Tropicana, Poets Princess	-683	+22835
1/5	**Delft Dancer W2/1**, Chantress, Double Reflection, **Precious Ramotswe W15/8**, Ramblow, Slow to Hand, **It's the Only Way 6/4**	+138	+23518
30/4	**Steeve W5/2**, Battle Lines	+150	+23380
29/4	Champagne Champ, **Highland Bobby 6/1**	+500	+23230
28/4	**Altior W1/4**, Midnight Shot, Recollect	-175	+22730
27/4	**Crystal Ocean W1/1, Dubhe W11/4**, Grinty, Humble Gratitude **Castletown W4/1**, Boric, **Jurby W3/1**, Bellandenall	+675	+22905
26/4	Cornerstone Lad, Some Are Lucky, Roll the Dough, Awake at Midnight Morney Wing, Inflexiball, Minella Tweet, Raucous, **Lunar Eclipse W7/4**	-625	+22230
25/4	Boom the Groom, Dee Ex Bee, **Calett Mad W11/10**, Thundering Home	-190	+22855
24/4	**Gumball W2/5**, Ut Majuer Aulmes, **Point N Shoot W15/8, Corrosive 7/2** Cubswin	+378	+23045
23/4	Atletico, Ingenuity, **Justforjames W11/4**	+75	+22667
22/4	**Blu Cavalier W5/4**	+125	+22592
21/4	Wasntexpectingthat, Warthog, Truckers Highway, Barney Dwan, Tizwotitiz	-500	+22467
20/4	Risk and Roll, **Skint W11/4**, Miss Tynte, Capard King, Spader, Expensive Liaison, Champagne Champ, Tigre Du Terre	-425	+22967
19/4	Le Brivido, Argentello, Occupy, Whatzdjazz, Havanna Star, **Hediddodinthe W2/1, Extra Mile W15/8**, Trump Alexander	-213	+23392
18/4	Ripley, BubbleaAnd Squeak, **Magic Dancer W6/1**	+400	+23605
16/4	**Bakht A Rawan W7/1**	+700	+23205
14/4	**Kimberlite Candy W3/1, Berkshire Royal W15/8**	+488	+22505
13/4	Vision Des Flos, Min, **Bennys Girl W2/1**, Broadway Belle, Coastal Cyclone	-200	+22017
12/4	Zoltan Varga, **Da Capo Dandy W9/4**	+125	+22217

Date	Selection	W/L	Totals
11/4	Shockingtimes, Perfect Hustler	-200	+22092
10/4	Run Don't Hide, Toolatetodelegate	-200	+22292
9/4	**Highway One O One W7/2, Kilfilum Cross W3/1, Ramore Will W5/2** Weebill, Fourth Act , **I'm A Game Changer W5/2, Jammin Masters W9/2,** The King's Steed	+1300	+22492
8/4	**Skywards Reward W2/1**, McGowans Pass, **Asking Questions W5/2**	+350	+21192
7/4	Dinsdale, **Secret Legacy W7/4**, Billy Hicks, **Ballyarthur W4/1**, Donna's Diamond, Tuscany	+175	+20842
6/4	**Norman The Red W7/1**	+700	+20667
3/4	The Jungle Vip	-100	+19967
2/4	**Bartholomeu Dias W4/11**	+36	+20067
1/4	Sartene's Son, **Mujassam W4/5, The Lion Dancer W6/4**	+130	+20031
31/3	Laughton, Eesha Beauty	-200	+19901
30/3	Oriental Lilly, Black Sails, **Izzer W15/8**, Quench Dolly	-112	+20101
29/3	Piton Pete, **The Bay Birch W5/4, Something Lucky W9/4**	+225	+20213
28/3	Harefield, Cadeau Du Bresil, Nature Boy, Harmonica	-400	+19988
27/3	Powerful Society	-100	+20388
26/3	**Or De Vassy W5/4**, Mount Rushmoore, **Clondaw Westie W8/1**	+825	+20488
25/3	Tonto's Spirit, Allmyown, Broderie	-300	+19663
24/3	Lancelot Du Lac, **Branscombe 4/1**, My Target, Oisrakh Le Noir, Waterlord, **Knockrobin W15/8, Vale of Kent W2/1**	+388	+19963
23/3	**Fire Fighting W 5.45**	+423	+19575
22/3	**Michaels Mount W1/4, 3.35 Silver Kayf W13/8,** Just Cameron, Lac Sacre Scribner Creek, Loyalty	-213	+19152
21/3	Midnight Shadow, **Skewiff W13/8**, Doc Carver, Epitaph, Silchester, Garran **Virginia Chick W6/1**	+263	+19365
20/3	Bobby K, Odds on Oli	-200	+19102
19/3	**Cliffs of Dover W10/11**	+91	+19302
17/3	Sao, Kilcrea Vale, **Behind Time W3/1**, Piri Massini, Society Ranger	-100	+19211
16/3	Urban Kode, **Bedrock W4/9**, Coopers Friend, Apple's Shakira, Saucysioux, Mortens Leam **Weebill W30/100**, Potters Legend, Crown Walk, New Orleans, **Carpet Time W4/6**	-659	+19311
15/3	Scotchtown, American Life, Cornerstone Lad, Turtle Cask, Achill Road Boy Bogart, Bold Prediction	-700	+19970

Date	Selection	W/L	Totals
14/3	Warriors Tale, **As I See It W11/10**	+10	+20670
13/3	**Big KittenW8/11**, Rockwood, Solid Man	-127	+20660
12/3	Sandhurst Lad	-100	+20787
11/3	**Piton Pete W5/4, Talk of The South W7/2**, Yourholidayisover Isabeg Lane, **Calipso Collonges W11/10**	+385	+20887
10/3	Quothquan Aimee Sivola, Fourth Act**, The Jam Man W11/10**, Harry Topper, Somchine, Desert Fox, Soldier in Action	-590	+20502
9/3	Kastani Beach, Charmant, Dedigout, Darkest Light, **Grandfather Tom 11/8**, Spirit of Zebedee	-363	+21092
8/3	**Craving W1/9**, Brother Tiger, Vieux Lille, **Grove Silver W5/2**, Cultram Abbey	-39	+21455
7/3	**Shine Baby Shine W8/1**, De Medici, **Herecomesthesun W13/8**, Fortunes Pearl	+763	+21494
6/3	Archimedes	-100	+20731
5/3	**Kuptana W8/15**, Leith Hill Legasi, Sartene's Son, Black Sails	-247	+20831
4/3	**Seasearch W9/4**, Best Tamayuz	+125	+21077
3/3	Yensir	-100	+20952
28/2	**Compatriot W4/5**	+80	+21052
27/2	**Walk in The Park 2/9**	+22	+20972
26/2	Angelina D'or, **Sotomayor W2/1, Sixties Idol 8/1, Greyed A W5/6**, Soulsaver, Bialco, **Bulls Head W7/4**, Surprise Vendor	+858	+20950
25/2	Royal Act, Thibault, Fergal Mael Duin, Call Me Sid, **The Flying Sofa W13/8**	-238	+20092
24/2	Fourth Act, Acdc, Densfirth, Big Time Maybe	-400	+20330
23/2	**Doctor Bartolo W7/4**, Calipto, **Talk of The South W11/4, Perfect Illusion 10/11**, Rowlestonerendezvu	+341	+20730
22/2	Mr Christopher, Silchester, Poyle Vinnie, **Great Return W3/1, Shining Romeo W7/1**, Alberta, Mr Witmore	+500	+20389
21/2	**Goohar W15/2, Two for Gold W3/1, Athollblair Boy 2/1**, Firefighting Little Palaver	+1050	+19889
20/2	Oscar Rose, The Kings Writ, Caid Du Lin, Unveiling, **Dark Alliance W15/8**	-212	+18839
19/2	Finnegans Garden, Coolking, **Blottos 11/8, Windsor Avenue 1/4**, Western Way	-138	+19051
18/2	Nansaroy, Streets of Promise, Dawnieriver	-300	+19189

Date	Selection	W/L	Totals
17/2	War Sound, **Brother Tiger W5/2**, Man of Harlech, Poetic Imagination, **Tommy Rapper 11/2**, Templeross, Lucymai, Gothic Empire	+200	+19489
16/2	**Rather Be 2/5**, Princeton Royale, Et Moi Aloris, Potters Legend, Evince, Alfonso Manana	-460	+19289
15/2	**Rons Dream W4/6, Mac N Cheese W8/1**, Dr Hooves, **Glance Back W7/4**, Timon's Tara, **Night of Glory 5/4**, Distingo, Harbour Patrol	+767	+19749
14/2	Bungee Jump, **Red Vernon W5/6**, Divine Spear, Titus Bolt, **Nendrum W4/1**, Midnight Glory, Harefield, Hunt Politics, Daltrey, **Great Return W4/5**	-37	+18982
12/2	Third Act	-100	+19019
11/2	Mercenaire, **Elegant Escape W10/11**	-9	+19119
10/2	Saphir Du Rheu, Duke Des Champs, Quids In, Sir Will, Helvetian, Dark Alliance	-600	+19128
9/2	**Happy Diva W11/10**, Applesolutely, Potterman, Bertie Barnes, **Bigbadjohn W5/2, Shamrokh 2/1, Heavens Guest W8/1**	+1060	+19728
8/2	**Marmont W5/2, Midnight Target W3/1**, Equus Secretus, Red Indian, Duelling Banjos, Poetic Imagination	+150	+18668
7/2	**Mossy Lodge W5/1**	+500	+18508
6/2	Master of Finance	-100	+18008
5/2	**Two Swallows 5/4**, Lex Talionis, **Beyondtemptation W7/2**, Rosquero	+275	+18108
4/2	**Culture De Sivola W10/1**, Carlton Ryan	+900	+17743
3/2	**Shambra W15/8**, Kayf Blanco, **Authors Dream W5/2, Aiya W7/4, Humbert W10/11**	+604	+16843
2/2	Don't Ask, **Rock My Style W6/5, Oak Vintage W11/4**, Timon's Tara Craving, **Watersmeet W4/7**, Captain Swift, **Petruchio W5/2**	+302	+16239
1/2	Le Boizelo, Hideaway Vic, Mr Christopher, **Pulsating W13/8**	-138	+15937
31/1	**Indian Reel W11/4**, Bekkensfirth, Time to Blossom, Shanroe Street, Vale of Kent, Poppy in The Wind	-225	+16075
30/1	Dichato, Casual Cavalier, **Lord County W11/10**, Filatore	-190	+16300
27/1	**Apple's Shakira W1/5**, Crank em Up, Intrepidly, **Wakanda W8/1**	+620	+16490
26/1	Dalkadam, **Wotziname 5/2**, Capard King, One of Us, **Age of Wisdom 2/5**, Ambient, **Attain W2/1**, Rebel Beat, Protek Des Flos, Cloth Cap	-210	+15870
25/1	Talk of The South, Crucial Role, Zylan, Epitaph, Zoravan **Cool Mix W4/9, Outlaw TornW5/1**, Tabernas, Mambo Dancer	-156	+16080
24/1	**Jaunty Flight DH6/5**, Dedigout, Notebook, **Power and Peace W10/11**, Mount Wellington	-149	+16236

Date	Selection	W/L	Totals
23/1	**Optimus Prime W1/3**, Sneaking Budge, **Captain Lars W11/10**, **Catarmaran Du Seil W6**/4	+193	+16385
22/1	Yourholidayisover, Rio Quinto, Morney Wing, Wish In A Well	-400	+16192
21/1	**Lisp W2/9**, 2.10 Theos Charm, George Dryden	-178	+16592
20/1	Chester Street, **Nayati 8/11**, Crossed My Mind, **Un De Sceaux 4/9**	-83	+16770
19/1	**Ramses De Teillee 13/8**, Swing Hard, Conkering Hero, Native Appeal	-138	+16853
18/1	Sunshineandbubbles, Luv U Whatever, Ochos Rios, **Happy Diva 1/1**	-200	+16991
17/1	**Whatswrongwithyou W2/1, Saint Calvados W11/8**, Black Lightning	+238	+17191
16/1	Handsome Sam, Gassini Golf, **Mercers W10/1**, Howardian Hills	+700	+16953
15/1	Well Smitten, Trust Thomas, Tomahawk Wood, Mythical Madness, **Mount Tahan W11/10**	-290	+16253
14/1	**Clondaw Castle W5/4**, Dexcite, Ange Des Malberaux, Bernardelli Snowy Winter, Kensington Star, Mr Coco Bean	-475	+16543
13/1	Equus Millar, **Black Ivory W5/1**, Secret Investor, The Tailger, Rothman, Surrey Hope, Qassem, Taste the Salt, Jaleo, Granville Island, Muthraab Aldaar, Monte Cinq, **Mr Carbonator W4/1**	-200	+17018
12/1	Bleu Et Noir, Freebie Rocks, **Dark Alliance W5/4**, Kingsley Klarion **Wazowski W4/1**, Frankie Ballou, Bulkov, First Du Charmil, Gumball, The British Lion, **Wiff Waff W5/4**	-150	+17218
11/1	**Dresden W7/2**, Zigger Zagger, Danzay, Tangramm, **Marshal Aid 9/2**	+500	+17368
10/1	**Zalvados W4/6**, Monbeg Oscar, Fortune and Glory, Make Music, Aibell, Spring Waterfall, Robbie Roo Roo	-533	+16868
9/1	Acker Bilk, Papa Stour, Tagur, Tasaaboq, Furni Factors, **Black Op W 4/7**, Black Tulip, Crystal Lad, **Kohuma W7/1**, As I See It, Orbasa, Unioniste	-243	+17401
8/1	**Greyed A W11/10**, Berlusca	+10	+17644
7/1	**Bramble Brook W6/4**, Whispering Harry	+50	+17634
6/1	Govenor's Choice, **Another Venture W5/2**, Court Frontier, **Good Boy Bobby W13/8, SperedekW 2/1**, Uhlan Bute, Dance Teacher, **Lord George W7/2, Choice Encounter W7/4**	+838	+17584
5/1	Top Break, Eljaddaaf	-200	+16746
4/1	Kaser, Thankyou Very Much, **Winds of Fire W8/11, Desert Ruler W9/2, DH Oneida Tribe 11/4**, Uppertown Prince, **Fin and Game W11/8** The British Lion, Gabriel The Terror, **Udontdodou W15/8**, Boom the groom, Exchequer, Red Invader	+187	+16946

Date	Selection	W/L	Totals
3/1	**Look My Way W1/4**, Sister Sybil, Sainte Ladylime, Kestrel Valley, Mullaghmurphy Blue, **Nendrum W9/2**, Toarmandowwithlove, **Mixboy W15/8**, Unnoticed, Bush Beauty	-37	+16759
2/1	Intisaab, Shamson, **Lord of the Glen W5/4**	-75	+16796
1/1/2018	Axe Cap, Here's Herbie, **Road to Milan W15/8**, Allee Bleue, **Yanworth W15/8, Acey Milan W100/30, More Than Luck W11/4**, Norse Light, Emma Beag, Dutch Canyon	+381	+16871
31/12	**Cailleach Annie W11/4**, Third Time Lucky, Shackled N Drawn, **Met by Moonlight W7/1**, Millicent Silver	+675	+16490
30/12	Reckless Endeavour, Line of Beauty, Acaro, **First Flow W6/4 Attest 9/4**, Gores Island	-25	+15815
29/12	Scotch Myst	-100	+15840
28/12	Sea Tee Dea, Ode to Autumn, Under Red Sky	-300	+15940
27/12	Haulani, **Tintern Theatre W4/1**, Run with Pride, Rizzle Drizzle, **Maratha W3/1**, Tasaaboq, **Just Cameron 10/1**, Archive	+1200	+16240
26/12	**Quick PickW15/8, Roxyfet W7/2**, Duhallowcountry, Rockalzaro, **Hit and Run W5/2**, Friendship Bay, Keel Haul, **Ellens Way W8/1**, Dick Darsie **W11/4**, Astracad, Wakanda, Trojan Star, **Bestwork W11/2**, Grageelagh Girl, **If You Say Run W1/2, Buveur D'air W1/5, Golan Fortune W15/2**	+2433	+15040
23/12	Barrys Jack, Born Survivor, **Ulbatique W4/1**, KK Lexion, Cap Du Nord Pougne Bobbi	-100	+12607
22/12	Georgieshore, **Chef Des Obeaux W2/5**, Brother Bennett, **Handsupfordetroit W9/1**, Best Tamayuz, Star Ascending, **Uncle Alastair W1/1**, Bullionaire, Mr Gent, **Champagne Pink W7/2**	+790	+12707
21/12	Good Time Ahead, **Hard Graft W10/1**, Vroom, Floral Banquet, The Cider Maker, Night of Sin, Tommy Rapper, **Complicit W2/1**	+600	+11917
20/12	Daybreak, Krazy Paving, Shanroe In Milan, Morello Royale, Melrose Boy, **Glencadam Master 13/8**, Pretty Bubbles	-438	+11317
19/12	Toarmandowwithlove, **Buckle Street W4/1**, Maxed Out King Handsome Dude, **Throckley 5/2**, Walsingham Grange	+250	+11435
18/12	**Silver Concorde W1/3**, Champagne Chaser, **Oxwich Bay W10/11**, **Potters Story W4/1**, Talk of The South, **Finnegans Garden W11/4, Hideaway Vic W4/6**, Purple Rock, **Ballymore Castle 8/11, Pure Shores W9/4**	+864	+11185
17/12	Mondo Cane, Glenn Coco, Dukes Meadow	-300	+10321
16/12	Cooking Fat, Mohaayed, Braqueur D'or	-300	+10621
15/12	Bernardelli, **Waterlord W1/2, Tawseef W5/2**	+300	+10921
14/12	**Our Merlin W7/4, 3.15 Dream Bolt W6/1**, Bezos, Dashing Dusty, **Mutawathea 6/1**	+1175	+10621

Date	Selection	W/L	Totals
13/12	Maratha, **Dutiful Son W1/1**, Haraz , **Take Two W8/1**, **Shyron W7/1**, Cadueax Boxer, **Sooqaan W6/1**, Mansfield, Lagenda, **Rouge Nuage 18/1** Azeitia, Dragon Dream, Viola Park	+3200	+9446
11/12	Fergal Mael Duin, Project Mars, **On the Warpath W4/6**	-133	+6246
9/12	Just A Sting, **Pop Rockstar 7/2**, Pistol Park, Le Breuil, **Chooseyourweapon 10/11**, **Millanisi Boy W8/1**, **Mr Reckless 6/1**, Spin Point, **Velvet Revolution W4/1**, **Soghan W11/4**	+2116	+6379
8/12	Lady Longshot, Modus, Coolking, Inniscastle Lad, Dick Darsie, **Viserion W3/1**, **Contented W1/1**, Court House, Loveatfirstsight	-300	+4263
7/12	Drinks Interval, Jennys Surprise, Chateau Robin, Mondo Cane, **Triopas W5/2**, Sibilance, **Glen Coco W 7/2**, Chaucers Tale, Hediddoninthe	-100	+4593
6/12	Summer Icon, Karam Albaari, **Royal Beekeeper W6/4**, Late Night Lily, **Schnabel W10/11**, **Pop Rockstar W100/30**, Morney Wing	+171	+4693
5/12	Castletown, Doctor Rex, Ben Arthur, **Point Hope W7/2**	+50	+4522
4/12	**Restive W8/11**, Siempre Amigos, Astrum, Craigmoor, **Saucysioux W4/9**, **Optimus Prime W8/11**, Culture De Sivola, **Solomon Grey W1/1**	-111	+4472
3/12	Laval Noir, Fox Appeal, Wind Place and Sho, Grand Courier, Bourne	-500	+4583
2/12	**Kalashnikov W8/11**, **Deauville Dancer W5/4**, Barlow, Cap Soleil, **Treshnish W7/2**, Bishops Road, Whispering Harry	+148	+5083
1/12	Luv U Whatever, Majestic Moon, Pearl Nation, **Shearin W11/2**, Seaview, **No CeilingW3/1**, **Manny Owens W100/30**, **Chapel Style W5/2**, Cyrname,	+930	+4935
	NOVEMBER 2017	+4005	+4005

Date	Selection	W/L	Totals
17/3	Larkbarrow Lad W 15/8	+188	+21915
16/3	Paper Promise W15/8, Corinto, The Captains Inn W6/4	+238	+21727
15/3	Unforgiving Minute 11/8, National Glory	+38	+21489
14/3	Paisley Park 7/4, Sense of Direction	+75	+21451
13/3	Finawn Bawn W1/2, Bbold, Ulster	-150	+21376
12/3	Exalted Angel, Camachess W13/8	+63	+21526
11/3	Red Force One, Fitzroy	-200	+21463
9/3	Captain Lars, Derrianna Spirit, Treacherous W4/1	+200	+21663
8/3	Air Force Army	-100	+21463
7/3	Vis A Vis, Green Dolphin W3/1, Christmas In Usa W6/5, Frisella W4/7	+377	+21563
6/3	Perfect Moment, Mortens Leam	-200	+21186
5/3	Juge Et Parti, Decoration of War	-200	+21386
4/3	Wanaasah	-100	+21586
1/3	Zmhar 4/7, Moonlight Spirit 1/4, The White Mouse 11/10	+192	+21686
28/2	Alright Sunshine W5/4, Blazon W6/4	+275	+21494
27/2	Champagne Mystery	-100	+21219
26/2	All Is Good, Bay of Naples W5/6	-17	+21319
25/2	Western Honour W11/10, Graasten, The Flying Sofa, The Cashel Man	-190	+21336
24/2	Shantou Flyer W8/11	+73	+21526
23/2	Cool Mix 4/6, Alkaamel W8/11	+138	+21453
22/2	Epatante 1/5, Reve 4/7, Straidnahanna, Top Power	-123	+21315
21/2	Ingleby Hollow W10/11, I'm To Blame W8/11, Clondaw Castle W10/11, Plumette	+155	+21438
20/2	Champagne Well, Doctor Dex W13/8	+63	+21283
18/2	Full Throttle W11/10	+110	+21220
17/2	Supakalanistic	-100	+21110
16/2	Road to Rome W13/8	+163	+21210
15/2	Sir Egbert, Kalashnikov, Elusive Belle, Elysees Palace, Lion Hearted 10/11 Orchid Star 1/7	-295	+21047
14/2	Dream Du Grand Val 4/7, We Have A Dream 2/5, Definitely Red, Inch Lala	-103	+21342
4/2	Southfield Stone, Marhaban W1/2	-50	+21445

Date	Selection	W/L	Totals
2/2	**Orchid Star W2/9**	+22	+21495
31/1	Eve Harrington	-100	+21473
30/1	Bobby Biscuit	-100	+21573
29/1	**Nestor Park W13/8**	+163	+21673
28/1	Extra Mag, Talkischeap, **Pym W8/13**	-138	+21510
27/1	Urbanist	-100	+21648
26/1	**Fearsome W1/1, Nubough W4/9**	+144	+21748
25/1	**Scarlet Dragon W2/1,** Magic of Light	+100	+21604
23/1	**St Peters Basilica 1/1,** Vandella, Kamra	-100	+21504
22/1	**Clondaw Castle W6/4**	+150	+21604
21/1	**Ingleby Hollow W15/8, Windsor Avenue W10/11**	+279	+21454
20/1	**Ask Ben 10/11**	+91	+21175
19/1	Redicean, **Probability W6/5**	+20	+21084
17/1	Humble Hero	-100	+21064
16/1	Woods	-100	+21164
14/1	**Whatswrongwithyou W4/7**, Umndeni, Mount Ararat	-143	+21264
13/1	Lord Yeats	-100	+21407
12/1	**Tough Remedy W6/4**	+150	+21507
11/1	Precious Bounty, **Rock Bottom W9/4**	+125	+21357
10/1	**Uno Mas W5/4,** Black Salt, **Brecon Hill 1/1**	+125	+21232
9/1	Secret Ace, **Diamond Gait W11/10**, Fox Appeal, Cenotaph	-190	+21107
8/1	**Two for Gold W10/11,** Frenchy Du Large, **Ribble Valley 5/4**	+116	+21297
7/1	**Ontopoftheword W2/5, Alright Sunshine 4/6,** Sevarano, **Given Choice W11/10**	+117	+21181
6/1	Oden	-100	+21064
5/1	**Laurina W1/7**	+14	+20264
4/1	**Clarendon Street W2/5,** Bastien, Skydiving	-160	+20250
3/1	**Capone W8/11, Weld Al Emarat W15/8**	+261	+20410
2/1	Royal Prospect	-100	+20149
1/1	Always Lion, Foxtrot Juliet	-200	+20249

Date	Selection	W/L	Totals
31/12	Gin Palace, Printing Dollars	-200	+20449
28/12	**Let Rip W5/4**	+125	+20649
27/12	**Altior W1/5**	+20	+20524
26/12	Schiehallion Munro	-100	+20504
22/12	Bingo D'Olivate	-100	+20604
21/12	Holiday Magic,**Vindication W4/6**	-33	+20704
20/12	Country 'n' Western	-100	+20737
19/12	Drinks Interval	-100	+20837
17/12	Lady Lizzie, **Anycity W3/1**	+200	+20937
16/12	**Earlofthecotswolds W4/7**, Xpo Universal, Rosie And Millie	-143	+20737
15/12	Newtown Boy, **Quel Destiny W10/11, O O Seven 6/4, Persian Sun 11/10** Late Shipment	+150	+20880
14/12	Pipes of Peace	-100	+20730
13/12	**Southfield Stone W30/100,** Jester Jet, Black Buble	-170	+20830
12/12	**Ebony Gale 6/4,** She Mite Bite, **Mainsail Athletic 6/4,** More Than More	+100	+21000
10/12	**Wolfcatcher W6/5,** Regal Banner	+20	+20900
7/12	Remastered, **Carnival Queen W10/11**	-8	+20880
6/12	Rocku	-100	+20888
5/12	Wirral Girl, **Newtide W7/4,** Al Messila	-25	+20988
4/12	Bang Bang Rosie	-100	+21013
2/12	Navajo War Dance, Barrys Jack	-200	+21113
1/12	Lorna Cole	-100	+21313
29/11	**Unblinking W13/8, Manorah W2/1**	+363	+21413
27/11	Et Moi Alors	-100	+21050
26/11	The Ogle Gogle Man	-100	+21150
24/11	Briyouni, Just Glamorous, Boagrius	-300	+21250
23/11	**Wenyourreadyfreddie W4/6**, Braavos, **Inhale 7/4**	+142	+21550
22/11	Dandolo Du Gite, **Cantiniere W10/11**	-9	+21408
20/11	Hill sixteen, Blottos, **My Mate Mark W9/4,** Spirit of Zebedee, **Earl of Bunnacurry W5/4, Watersmeet W11/4**	+325	+21417
18/11	The Lincoln Lawyer, Morney Wing, Arquebusier, Dynamite Dollar	-400	+21092

Date	Selection	W/L	Totals
17/11	**Barys W3/1**, Skidoosh, Ravens Tower, One of Us	Level	+21492
16/11	Uncle Jerry, Lucymai	-200	+21492
15/11	Annie Bonny	-100	+21692
14/11	Anytime Now, Al Destoor	-200	+21792
12/11	Lexington Law	-100	+21992
10/11	**Donjuan Triumphant W3/1, Bags Groove W5/4**	+425	+22092
9/11	**Elysees W4/5, Windsor Avenue W1/3, Weather Front 11/10,** Sounds of Italy	+123	+21667
8/11	**Informateur 4/7,** Posh Trish	-43	+21544
6/11	**Leodis Dream W4/5, Nivaldo W7/4**	+255	+21587
5/11	Milldean Star	-100	+21332
4/11	Cyrname	-100	+21432
3/11	Smugglers Creek	-100	+21532
2/11	Denmead	-100	+21632
1/11	**Champagne to Go W100/30**	+333	+21732
31/10	Movewiththetimes	-100	+21399
30/10	**Anytime Will Do W5/4**, Boy in A Bentley, Doctor Dex, Kings Highway	-175	+21499
29/10	Quri, **Scheu Time 1/6**, Vincent's Forever	-183	+21674
27/10	**Young Rascal W5/4, Dinons W10/11**	+154	+21857
26/10	Franz Kafka, Court Minstrel, Bang on Frankie, Verve	-400	+21703
25/10	Stowaway Magic, Zabeel Star, Agamemmon, Royal Ruby	-400	+22103
24/10	Rapper, **Morney Wing W3/1**	+200	+22503
23/10	Maqsad, **Nashirah W6/5**, Cadeau Magnifique, Gorham's Cave	-180	+22303
22/10	Dream Machine, Seventi, Call to Order, Gifts of Gold, Blue Mountain	-500	+22483
21/10	**Verdana Blue W5/6**	+83	+22983
20/10	**Ice Gala W4/9**, Etamine Du Cochet	-56	+22900
19/10	Bardd, Barys, **Boston George W6/4**	-50	+22956
18/10	**Karnavaal W7/4**, Muneyra	+75	+23006
17/10	Deebee	-100	+22931
16/10	**What's Occurring W5/2**	+250	+23031
15/10	Tarboosh, **Jahbath W8/11**	-27	+22781

Date	Selection	W/L	Totals
13/10	Monbeg Legend, Sneaky Feeing, Rock the Kasbah, Baydar, El Gumryah	-500	+22808
11/10	**Awake at Midnight 11/10**	+110	+23308
10/10	**McGroarty 5/4, Sovereign Grant W15/8**, Elector	+213	+23198
9/10	Prestbury Park	-100	+22985
8/10	**Lungarno Palace W13/8**, Gloweth	+63	+23085
7/10	Vaniteux	-100	+23022
6/10	Our Three Sons, Holmeswood	-200	+23122
5/10	Great Beyond	-100	+23322
3/10	**Clara Peters W9/2**, Louie De Palma, **Wandrin Star W3/1**	+650	+24322
2/10	Caid Du Lin, Brave Spartacus, Panko	-300	+23672
1/10	**Green or Black 9/4, On Demand 6/4**	+375	+23972
30/9	**Nate The Great W2/5**	+20	+23597
29/9	**Barristan The Bold W9/4**, African Ride	+125	+23577
28/9	Unforgetable Filly, Elegiac	-200	+23452
27/9	Make A Wish, **Global Jackpot W4/5**, Cockley Beck, Drill, Buffalo River, Elector	-420	+23652
26/9	London Protocol, **Master Carpenter W7/2, Make My Heart Fly W1/1**	+350	+24072
25/9	Welsh Lord	-100	+23722
24/9	Happy Power, **Faro Angel 5/6,** Forest View, Smashing Lass	-217	+23822
22/9	**Anasheed W6/5, Swordbill W5/4**, Shumookhi	+145	+24049
21/9	Quite by Chance, Scoop the Pot, **Dirty Rascal W11/10**, Beat Le Bon	-190	+23904
20/9	Sky Patrol, Boerham, Silvery Moon, **Baritone W1/2**	-250	+24094
19/9	Sovereign Grant, **Encore D'Or 5/4**	+25	+24344
18/9	Harpelle	-100	+24319
17/9	**Stacey Sue 1/1, Baltic Prince 7/2, Kamikaze Lord 4/6**	+418	+24419
15/9	Daphinia, Oh This Is Us, Spray the Sea	-300	+24001
14/9	**Swift and Sure W6/5**	+120	+24301
13/9	Fox Fearless, Tolkyn	-200	+24181
11/9	Val Mome, **Quicksand W1/1**	Level	+24381
10/9	Good Tyne Girl	-100	+24381
9/9	Nordican Bleue, Desiremoi D'Authie	-200	+24481

Date	Selection	W/L	Totals
8/9	**Innocent Touch 9/4, Rene Mathis 9/4**	+450	+24681
7/9	Gallic, Bangkok, **Sky Defender 10/11**, Mainsail Atlantic, Alfurat River	-309	+24231
6/9	**Peppay Le Pugh W8/11,** Volcanic Sky	-27	+24540
5/9	**Beat That W2/7, Angel of Harlem W4/5,** Silver Crescent	+9	+24567
4/9	**Henry Smith 4/7,** Agreement	-43	+24558
3/9	**Dirty Rascal W10/11,** Prabeni, **Hard Taskmaster W5/6**	+74	+24601
2/9	Archie	-100	+24527
1/9	**Leapaway W1/3,** Bertog, Leroy Leroy	-167	+24627
31/8	**Captain Peacock W1/1, Kingston W9/2, Muthhila W6/5,** Theatre of War	+570	+24794
30/8	Federal Law, Blackheath	-200	+24224
28/8	**Romaana W1/3, Maaward W5/4**	+158	+24424
27/8	**Indian Viceroy W1/2, Ormesher 11/8**	+188	+24266
26/8	The Big Bad	-100	+24078
25/8	Look Around, **Nayef Road 11/10, Expert Eye 5/4,** Island Song	+35	+24178
24/8	Momkin, **Stradivarius 4/11**	-64	+24143
23/8	**Lah Ti Dar W1/1,** Rawdaa, **Longhouse Sale 2/5**	+40	+24207
21/8	**Choco Box W1/1**	+100	+24167
20/8	Petrastar	-100	+24067
19/8	Gustav Mahler	-100	+24167
18/8	**Missy Mischief W13/8, Caius Marcus W4/1**	+563	+24267
17/8	**Lovin W6/4,** Cat Royale	+50	+23704
16/8	**Glass Slippers W5/4,** Courtside	+25	+23654
15/8	**Cracker Factory W1/5,** Desirable Court	-80	+23629
13/8	**It's the Only way W4/7**	+57	+23709
12/8	Recollect, **Perfect Symphony W4/1**	+300	+23662
11/8	Toffee Galore, **Forward Thinking W9/2**	+350	+23362
10/8	Desert Lantern	-100	+23012
8/8	**Ventura Ocean W11/8,** Shouranour, Reverend Jacobs, Trouble and Strife, **Laith Alereen 5/4, Letmestopyouthere W5/6**	+146	+23112
7/8	Al Mortajaz	-100	+22966
5/8	**The Trader W11/10,** Rockin Roy, Ezanak	-90	+23066

Date	Selection	W/L	Totals
4/8	Major Partnership W2/7, Branscombe W4/1	+429	+23156
3/8	Mankib W6/4, Get Ready Freddy, Haadhir	-50	+22727
2/8	Alexander the Grey, Arigato W8/11	-27	+22777
1/8	Angels Envy, Rathbone, Poets Dawn, Takiah	-400	+22804
31/7	Youghal By the Sea W5/6	+83	+23204
30/7	Twister, Wavepoint 100/30	+230	+23121
28/7	Gabriel The Wire, Baronial Pride, Star of The East W 5/4	-75	+22891
27/7	Ascended, I'lletyougonow, Timoshenko W8/11, Fairlight W8/11	-55	+22966
26/7	The Last but One W5/6, Little Windmill W10/1, Arabian Jazz, Gripper, Right Direction W10/11	+974	+23021
25/7	Bayshore Freeway W4/5, Solesmes W15/8, Heartwarming W2/5, Clenymistra	+208	+22047
24/7	IAdvanced Hero W8/13, Mayassar W8/13, Sanam	+23	+21839
23/7	Axe Axelrod, Queen Jo Jo 8/11	-27	+21816
22/7	Cotton Club, Ornua W4/6, Leapaway W1/3, Grey Spirit W11/10	+110	+21843
21/7	Partmership W8/13	+62	+21733
20/7	Loch Ness Monster W4/7, Showout W1/3	+90	+21671
19/7	Rockin Boy 4/7	+57	+21581
18/7	Deia Glory W1/1, Persian Moon W11/8	+238	+21524
17/7	Passing Call W1/1	+100	+21286
16/7	Magical Wish W1/1	+100	+21186
14/7	Mill Green W1/4, Bedouin's Story W10/11, Woodside Wonder 1/1	+216	+21086
13/7	Semoun W6/5, Alpha Centauri W4/9	+164	+20870
11/7	Trouble and Strife W5/6, Pink Iceburg W1/1, Shyjack Watheeqa W1/3	+216	+20706
10/7	Herculean W2/5	+40	+20490
9/7	Weightfordave W5/6	+83	+20450
7/7	Thriving W5/6	+83	+20367
4/7	Skin Deep W8/11, Vale of Kent W6/5, Altra VitaW 8/11, Groveman W8/11	+338	+20284
3/7	Brexit Time W11/8, The Great Wall W11/8, Matchmaking W4/7	+202	+19946
2/7	Construct W10/11, I Believe You W11/8	+229	+19744
1/7	Celestial Path W6/4, Fair Mountain W4/9, Leapaway 9/4, Perseid, Argentello 4/9	+364	+19515

Date	Selection	W/L	Totals
29/6	Blonde Warrior 2/5	+40	+19151
28/6	Desert Fire W10/11	+91	+19111
26/6	Victory Command W1/10, On A May Day W 1/3	+43	+19020
23/6	Crystal Ocean 4/7	+57	+18977
21/6	Shailene W4/6, Big Time Maybe W4/9	+44	+18920
19/6	Crageelagh Girl W4/5, Sea Youmzain	-20	+18876
18/6	Society Queen W4/6	+67	+18896
17/6	White Light, Gumriyah W10/11	-9	+18829
16/6	Chaleur 4/6	+67	+18838
15/6	Settie Hill W4/6	+67	+18771
14/6	Sea of Class W2/5, L'Inganno Felice W4/7	+97	+18704
12/6	Mutafani W4/11	+36	+18607
11/6	Kilfinichen Bay	-100	+18373
10/6	Tarboosh	-100	+18473
7/6	Blonde Warrior W4/9, Marylin W1/1, Soldiers Call W4/6, Bashiba, Savaanah W4/5	+291	+18573
6/6	Red Mist W8/11	+73	+18282
2/6	Royal Brave, Shaybani W4/5	+80	+18209
1/6	Eeh Bah Gum W1/1	+100	+18129
30/5	Northwest Frontier W10/11	+91	+17129
29/5	Ledham W4/6	+67	+17038
24/5	Poet's WordW 4/6	+67	+16971
23/5	Bailarico W6/4, Jawal W11/10	+110	+16904
20/5	Tigre Du Terre W1/4, Miss Adventure W4/6	+92	+16794
19/5	Queen of Bermuda W4/6, Purser W6/4	+217	+16702
18/5	Al Muffrih W13/8	+163	+16485
16/5	Harry Angel 4/7, Champ 1/7	+71	+16322
15/5	Deep Intrigue W4/5, Settie Hill 1/7	+94	+16251
5/5	Fujaira Prince W10/11	+91	+16157
2/5	Tin Hat W4/6	+67	+16066
1/5	It's the Only Way 6/4	+150	+15999

Date	Selection	W/L	Totals
28/4	Altior W1/4	+25	+15849
27/4	Crystal Ocean W1/1	+100	+15824
25/4	Calett Mad W11/10	+110	+15724
24/4	Gumball W2/5	+40	+15614
23/4	Ingenuity	-100	+15574
22/4	Blu Cavalier W5/4	+125	+15674
16/4	Bakht A Rawan W7/1	+700	+15549
14/4	Berkshire Royal W15/8	+188	+14849
12/4	Zoltan Varga, Da Capo Dandy W9/4	+125	+14661
11/4	Shockingtimes, Perfect Hustler	-200	+14536
10/4	Run Don't Hide, Toolatetodelegate	-200	+14736
8/4	Skywards Reward W2/1, McGowans Pass	+100	+14936
6/4	Norman The Red W7/1	+700	+14836
3/4	The Jungle Vip	-100	+14136
2/4	Bartholomeu Dias W4/11	+36	+14236
1/4	Sartene's Son, Mujassam W4/5, The Lion Dancer W6/4	+130	+14227
31/3	Eesha Beauty	-100	+14097
30/3	Izzer W15/8	+188	+14197
29/3	The Bay Birch W5/4	+125	+14009
27/3	Powerful Society	-100	+13884
26/3	Or De Vassy W5/4	+125	+13984
22/3	Michaels Mount W1/4, 3.35 Silver Kayf W13/8, Scribner Creek	+188	+13859
21/3	Skewiff W13/8	+163	+13671
19/3	Cliffs of Dover W10/11	+91	+13508
16/3	Weebill W30/100, Time W4/6	+97	+13417
14/3	Warriors Tale, As I See It W11/10	+10	+13320
13/3	Big KittenW8/11, Rockwood, Solid Man	-127	+13310
12/3	Sandhurst Lad	-100	+13337
11/3	Piton Pete W5/4, Calipso Collonges W11/10	+235	+13437
10/3	The Jam Man W11/10	+110	+13202

Date	Selection	W/L	Totals
9/3	Grandfather Tom 11/8	+138	+13092
8/3	Craving W1/9	+11	+12954
7/3	Herecomesthesun W13/8, Fortunes Pearl	+63	+12943
6/3	Archimedes	-100	+12880
5/3	Kuptana W8/15, Sartene's Son, Black Sails	-147	+12980
4/3	Seasearch W9/4, Best Tamayuz	+125	+13127
28/2	Compatriot W4/5	+80	+13002
27/2	Walk in The Park 2/9	+22	+12922
26/2	Greyed A W5/6	+83	+12900
25/2	The Flying Sofa W13/8	+163	+12817
23/2	Perfect Illusion10/11	+91	+12654
21/2	Athollblair Boy 2/1	+200	+12563
20/2	Dark Alliance W15/8	+188	+12363
19/2	Blottos 11/8, Windsor Avenue 1/4	+163	+12175
16/2	Rather Be 2/5	+40	+12012
15/2	Rons Dream W4/6, Night of Glory 5/4	+192	+11972
14/2	Red Vernon W5/6	+83	+11780
11/2	Elegant Escape W10/11	+91	+11697
9/2	Happy Diva W11/10	+110	+11606
6/2	Master of Finance	-100	+11496
5/2	Two Swallows 5/4	+125	+11596
4/2	Culture De Sivola W10/1	+1000	+11471
3/2	Shambra W15/8, Kayf Blanco, Authors Dream W5/2, Aiya W7/4, Humbert W10/11	+604	+10471
2/2	Rock My Style W6/5, Watersmeet W4/7	+121	+9867
1/2	Pulsating W13/8	+163	+9746
30/1	Dichato, Casual Cavalier, Lord County W11/10, Filatore	-190	+9583
27/1	Apple's Shakira W1/5, Crank em Up, Intrepidly, Wakanda W8/1	+620	+9773
26/1	Age of Wisdom 2/5	+40	+9153
25/1	Cool Mix W4/9	+44	+9113

Date	Selection	W/L	Totals
24/1	Notebook, **Power and Peace W10/11**, Mount Wellington	-109	+9069
23/1	**Optimus Prime W1/3**, Sneaking Budge, **Captain Lars W11/10, Catarmaran Du Seil W6**/4	+193	+9178
21/1	**Lisp W2/9**	+22	+8985
20/1	**Nayati 8/11**, Crossed My Mind, **Un De Sceaux 4/9**	+17	+8963
19/1	**Ramses De Teillee 13/8**, Swing Hard, Conkering Hero, Native Appeal	-138	+8946
18/1	**Happy Diva 1/1**	+100	+9084
17/1	**Whatswrongwithyou W2/1, Saint Calvados W11/8**, Black Lightning	+238	+8984
15/1	**Mount Tahan W11/10**	+110	+8856
14/1	**Clondaw Castle W5/4**	+125	+8746
10/1	**Zalvados W4/6**	+67	+8621
9/1	**Black Op W 4/7**	+57	+8554
8/1	**Greyed A W11/10**, Berlusca	+10	+8497
7/1	**Bramble Brook W6/4**, Whispering Harry	+50	+8487
6/1	Govenor's Choice, **Another Venture W5/2, Bobby W13/8, Choice Encounter W7/4**	+488	+8437
5/1	Top Break	-100	+7949
4/1	**Winds of Fire W8/11, Fin and Game W11/8**	+200	+8049
3/1	**Look My Way W1/4, Mixboy W15/8**	+213	+7849
2/1	**Lord of the Glen W5/4**	+125	+7636
1/1/2018	**Road to Milan W15/8, Yanworth W15/8**	+376	+7511
31/12	**Cailleach Annie W11/4**, Third Time Lucky, Shackled N Drawn, **Met by Moonlight W7/1**	+775	+7135
30/12	**First Flow W6/4**	+150	+6360
26/12	**Quick PickW15/8, Buveur D'air W1/5**	+245	+6210
22/12	**Chef Des Obeaux W2/5, Uncle Alastair W1/1**	+140	+5956
21/12	**Complicit W2/1**	+200	+5816
20/12	**Glencadam Master 13/8**	+163	+5616
18/12	**Silver Concorde W1/3, Oxwich Bay W10/11, Ballymore Castle 8/11**	+197	+5453
15/12	Bernardelli, **Waterlord W1/2, Tawaseef W5/2**	+200	+5256
14/12	**Our Merlin W7/4, Dream Bolt W6/1**	+775	+5056

Date	Selection	W/L	Totals
13/12	**Dutiful Son W1/1**, Haraz	Level	+4281
11/12	**On the Warpath W4/6**	+67	+4281
9/12	**Chooseyourweapon 10/11**	+91	+4214
8/12	**Contented W1/1**	+100	+4123
6/12	Summer Icon, **Schnabel W10/11**	-9	+4023
4/12	**Restive W8/11, Saucysioux W4/9, Optimus Prime W8/11, Solomon Grey W1/1**	+289	+4032
3/12	Fox Appeal	-100	+3743
2/12	**Kalashnikov W8/11, Deauville Dancer W5/4**	+198	+3843
30/11	**Diese Des Bieffes W4/9, Silver Concorde W8/13,** Potters Midnight, **Breathoffreshair W1/1**	+106	+3645
27/11	Bright Tomorrow, Dance Floor King	-200	+3539
25/11	**Carp Kid W13/8, Hit the Beat W15/8, Hipster Boy W6/4**	+501	+3037
24/11	**Apollo Creed W1/1,** Juge Et Parti, **Breathoffreshair W5/2,** Thello	+150	+2536
23/11	**Tranquil Star W8/11**	+73	+2386
19/11	**Fox Norton W10/11**	+91	+2313
17/11	**Big Baz W4/5**	+80	+2222
14/11	**Arthurs Gift W15/8, Jubulani W6/4**	+338	+2142
13/11	**Nuts Well W1/1,** Red Touch	Level	+1804
12/11	**Bredon Hill Lad W7/2,** Theatre Stage, **Houblon Des Obeaux W4/1**	+650	+1804
11/11	Achille, **Modus W4/6, Louis Vac Pouch W5/2**	+217	+1154
10/11	**Evies Wish W6/4, Have a Dream W10/11**	+241	+937
8/11	**Kascade W3/1,** Casemates Square	+200	+696
7/11	**Awesome Allan W15/8, Magic Mirror W11/4, Bow Street W1/3**	+496	+496

Made in the USA
Lexington, KY
24 June 2019